DIVE IN

Lessons learnt since Business school

DIVE IN
Lessons learnt since business school

RAEL BRICKER

B⫯I⫯B
Batya Bricker

Published by Batya Bricker Book Projects
Batya@batyabricker.co.za

Copyright © Rael Bricker 2018

Cover design, typeset and illustrations by Patricia Crain and Empressa
Printed and bound by IngramSpark.

ISBN 978-0-6483111-0-2

DEAR READER,

This is the book I have always wanted to write.

After attending the Mortgage and Finance Association of Australia (MFAA) convention in May 2015 as a guest speaker, I got on the plane back to Perth and contemplated the feedback. The positive reception from these talks spurred me on. By the time I got to Perth I had put almost 2000 words down.

A few weeks later 'Rael Bricker – Give your business the EDGE' was born as a keynote and workshop seminar business. The topics are broadly based around the material in this book and my blog, and weave a set of real-life experiences and stories into the theory.

The business school education of the 1980s was designed to teach a little about a lot of things. I was exposed to many aspects of business, but none in real depth. The MBA (or at least when I did it) is designed to prepare people for corporate executive positions. It was not a training ground for entrepreneurs. This book is about what I have learnt since – the mistakes and missteps, the successes and wins.

Most roles, lessons, and therefore examples in this book relate to my business experience, which is mostly around the business-to-consumer space. But through my presentations to varying organisations, I have seen that the challenges faced by small or medium business entrepreneurs, and their teams, are no different to large corporate entities.

My passion for public speaking also presents an opportunity for me to give back. To give back my experience and hopefully some knowledge, so that others can use that help towards their success in business.

I've missed more than 9000 shots in my career. I've lost almost 300 games. I've been trusted to take the game winning shot 26 times and missed. I've failed over and over and over again in my life. And that is why I succeed.

– M<small>ICHAEL</small> J<small>ORDAN</small>

I am often inspired by wise words from the past. Interspersed in this book will be a number of those quotes. If you like what you read and want a daily dose, find me at

Facebook: Rael Bricker

LinkedIn: Rael Bricker

Twitter: raybri

RB

DEDICATION

This book is dedicated to my family.

I am eternally grateful to Rafi – my rock, my strength and my guidance. It takes great courage when your husband of six months comes home and says that he is giving up his good job to go out on a limb and become an entrepreneur.

I could not ask for a better partner to share the journey.

Aimee, Jess and Michael have been my inspiration. It's been an amazing journey being able to share my life and my experiences and hopefully pass on a legacy to my children.

My parents who spent many years, despite my father's illness, working incredibly hard to provide for the family.

My father Aubrey z'l who died too early, gave me the courage and skills to stand up and speak.

CONTENTS

When I was 5 years old, my mother would tell me that happiness was the key to life. When I went to school, they asked me what I wanted to be when I grew up. I wrote down 'happy'. They told me I didn't understand the assignment, and I told them they didn't understand life.

JOHN LENNON

I don't want to get to the end of my life and find that I just lived the length of it. I want to have lived the width of it as well.

DIANE ACKERMAN

CHAPTER 1:

WHY

≋

It's December 2012, and I am standing on a beach north of Perth, in triathlon shorts, wearing a pink swimming cap, and wondering what had possessed me. I was about to start my first triathlon and finally realised that in all my training, I had never done a swim in the sea. Never mind one in a competitive field of a few hundred athletes.

You can never cross the ocean until you have the courage to lose sight of the shore.

ATTRIBUTED TO CHRISTOPHER COLUMBUS

So, it was with that courage, confidence (and a little craziness) that I ran into the sea, hopefully looking like a seasoned professional triathlete. Actually, it was pretty unlikely that I looked like any level of professional!

In a pool, you generally swim in an orderly line, swimming a set distance behind the next person and watching the black line on the bottom. The challenge of an open water swim is that you are swimming in a washing machine, being kicked from all sides, and constantly feeling your legs kicking others.

I did manage the swim and the triathlon, albeit in a very slow time. At the end the achievement was knowing that I had conquered it, despite the lack of sufficient training.

This moment, this approach, pretty much represents my approach to most things. We cannot prepare for every challenge in life. We need to have enough confidence in ourselves to know that when we do meet challenge, we can rise to it and conquer.

My late father often related the words of Henry Ford when he was asked about the secret of his success. He answered *'always jump at the good opportunities'*. The interviewer continued to ask how he identified these good opportunities. Ford replied, *'man, you just keep jumping.'*

My key business drivers are no different. Sometimes you can't be fully prepared for every challenge, but you have the confidence to take it on and make it work.

It is not the strongest of the species that survive, nor the most intelligent, but the one most responsive to change.

CHARLES DARWIN

Confidence is the key. It has taken the better part of my 54 years to understand and moderate the difference between self-confidence, over confidence and arrogance. Sometimes I still fall into the trap of mixing these up.

Over the course of this book I will reflect on times when I could have done things differently, perhaps better, but most certainly differently. More importantly, I see reflection as a way to learn and grow, not to control regrets.

In Larry E Greiner's paper *'Evolution and Revolution as Organizations Grow'* Greiner asserts that in order for any business to grow, it must face a number of crises. It taught me that in any process of evolution or development there needs to be a revolution. Embracing the crisis is, of course, essential to the successful process of change. This first crisis as defined by Greiner is often one of control and therefore this too has evolved to be a core business principle.

CHANGE IS GOOD – TAKE ON THE CHALLENGE

I try to embrace change for what it is – a time to reflect on how much better, or perhaps differently, we can do things.

I also sometimes fall into the trap of what I call the 'when we' mindset. As a South African migrant to Australia, I am often amused by those who instead of adapting to the new country, continually refer to 'when we were in South Africa, we ...' History is critical to shaping who we are in the future, but embracing and enjoying change is the challenge that allows us to grow.

WORKING LIFE

To lay a foundation for this book, I provide a summary of my working life so that the stories in the book can be placed into some chronology:

We did not grow up in a poor household, but disposable income was limited, so I needed to work to earn additional spending money for myself.

My first job was in retail sales at a 'mine store' called Hercules Trading, given to me by my father's cousin as a favour. In those days a 'mine store' was primarily aimed at serving predominantly black mine workers. They had two stores, one on the shaft at Hercules Shaft close to Johannesburg and another across from the taxi station at Alexandra Township. Alexandra was the less well-known of the two black defined living areas in Apartheid South Africa (Soweto was the other one). I worked there for a few weeks over one of my holidays when I was 13. I remember that as a privileged white South African, with limited exposure to the majority black population, I was now working behind the counter serving an almost exclusively black clientele. I have vivid memories of women coming into the store to buy staple food such as maize meal and reaching into their bra for the cash to make payment.

My next real job was at 15 at Hamrad Electronics in counter sales, and I also started a business installing car music systems. That business venture soon failed – my belief in my ability to work with my hands far exceeded the reality! But the resultant life lesson has significantly affected my future path.

In second year university I started my next business. I had business cards and it had a semi-professional look to it. *Reckless Rhythm – Mobile Disco and Musician Hire* lasted a few years while I was at university and provided a sporadic income. I still have boxes of vinyl singles gathering dust in my garage.

As I approached the end of my schooling, it became clear that I would need financial assistance to pursue a university degree. I was offered two scholarships, one from Armscor (a military equipment manufacturer) and the other from Anglo American Corporation. I chose the latter as I felt it to be a slightly better cultural fit for me (Armscor was strongly aligned with the mostly Afrikaans Government of the day). During university holidays, we were given jobs by Anglo American and were actually paid really well, as if we were in 'real jobs'.

At the completion of final year (fourth year) of my undergraduate degree in Electrical Engineering, and after various work experiences, I joined Vaal Reefs as a Junior Engineer, and then later Anglo American Head Office to work in the Control Systems Department. After six months at head office I resigned to go to business school full time to complete the first year of my MBA. At the same time, I completed my Masters in Software Engineering.

In mid-1990, I resigned from a small specialised software company called Kenwalt to start my own company called Innovative Management Development or IMD. It later morphed into 'IMD Education Centres'. My partner Jon Feldman and I had some grandiose plans for two young MBA graduates trying to teach the world how to run their businesses.

IMD grew rapidly, with the opening of offices in Johannesburg (head office), Durban, Cape Town, George, Wilderness and Lenasia. During mid-1996 we created an opportunity to sell the business to a small listed education and software company called AdVtech. We were then actively involved in acquisitions and expansion for the AdVtech Group. At the time I was also appointed as Managing Director of the MAST group, a computer training and education company controlled by AdVtech.

During August 1997, I resigned and took Rafi and our two daughters Aimee, aged three and Jessica, almost one, on a round-the-world trip for almost five months. On the 8th July 1999, Rafi and I embarked on our adventure to Australia.

In late July 1999 I was offered a position as Investment Manager for a small pooled development fund called Loftus Capital. (Another structure of a Venture Capital Fund). In December 2000 I was part of the team that listed the fund on the ASX (Australian Stock Exchange) after a successful capital raising.

To live without risk is to risk not living.

POPE PIUS XII

By July 2001, I decided that I needed to be an entrepreneur again, and tried my hand at being an importer. My good friend Brian Appleton from South Africa had found a product out of Germany that was an innovative storage solution for CDs. In an information-hungry age, it made sense to have a filing and storage system that could adequately store away CDs (and DVDs) in an easy-to-use orderly system.

We bought close to $50 000 worth of stock and I started marketing this through a variety of channels. Only then did I realise that being able to sell products into the retail channels in Australia required, in the main, being an accredited vendor to the various chains. As a single product company this proved to be near impossible. Apparently selling product was not really my game, and a few years later I managed to offload the stock for $5 000 after paying warehousing and other costs for many years.

During that same period, I reverted to venture capital work, looking for clients that I could assist in capital raising. Then a few clients asked me to raise some debt for them (as opposed to equity). Essentially companies have two ways to be funded, through debt (loans) or equity. The latter is either through investment in the business or retained profits from previous years.

At the time I had no idea how to get debt (loans) and discovered that I needed to be licensed in Western Australia as a finance Broker. I had no idea what a finance broker actually did, but, I got licensed and started to learn about raising debt for clients.

It transpired that I was reasonably good at this and clients started asking whether I could fix up their home loans too. Out of this (originally Mansion Capital) was the start of what is today the House & Home loans group. I had found my niche in being able to establish myself as a finance broker.

When Jon Feldman, my partner from IMD in South Africa joined the business (he needed to invest in a business in Australia to get his residency visa), we rebranded as House & Home Loans.

In 2004 we were approached by a property sales and support organisation called 'The Investors Club' to be one of their preferred brokers in Western Australia, and by extension, nationally. This provided a significant source of leads and property sales in the period from 2004 to 2008/9 when the GFC (global financial crisis) began to bite and sales slowed down. It was during that period in 2007 that Jon decided to sell his share in the business back to me, as he no longer wanted to be a finance broker. Since then I have been the sole shareholder in the group.

In 2009, Warren Dworcan, whom I had recruited as a broker, approached me with an idea to actively pursue lead generation through the internet. We agreed on a structure where I would receive a stake in Rate Detective Finance in the event of a sale or listing of the business. Collectively the two brands operated under one license with one set of overheads. The benefit, besides the lowering of operational costs, was that the combined loan volume earned us the ear of the lenders, something we probably would not have achieved as individual businesses. In 2014 Warren indicated that he wanted to open his own office and moved out of our premises in 2015.

In 2010, with Craig Shainfeld, we started House & Home Life. The aim was to provide a complimentary service to our clients through a financial planning business offering mostly risk (insurance) and Superannuation advice. Eighteen months later Craig was offered a position by a large eastern states financial planning business to run their WA operations. He accepted this position and during that year Ben Levy and Warren Kotkis joined House & Home Life. Today they are shareholders and directors of this business.

Over the past 17 years the collective group has settled more than $2.8bn in loans, mostly in the residential sector. The group and individuals in the group have won numerous awards and made many prestigious lists (such as top 25 Brokerages and Top 100 Brokers). The House & Home Loans Group is regarded as one of the leading brokerages in Australia.

CHAPTER 2

TIPS AND TRAPS – A BIRD'S EYE VIEW

> *People who don't take risks generally make about two big mistakes a year.*
>
> *People who do take risks generally make about two big mistakes a year.*
>
> PETER F. DRUCKER

The key tips and traps are woven into the fabric of this book. To give you a bird's eye view, this chapter presents them in the order that they were presented originally. They are not ranked in any order specifically, but should be read as independent ideas.

The points under each tip do not necessarily cover all the material related to that tip. Rather I have taken one small slice of the idea to put the tip into context. The rest of the book will offer many other examples that will add depth, dimensions and applications to these tips.

TIP 1: NEVER ASK STAFF TO DO ANYTHING YOU WOULD NOT DO

In starting and running an organisation, you need to be on top of each and every potential aspect of the business. There are many things I don't do anymore in the businesses, as I have staff to fulfil these roles. But I always bear in mind that if need be, I could do that job. These tasks range from the complex, related to specific aspects of the business through to the mundane, such as offering and making tea and coffee for clients and fellow staff members.

TIP 2: PEOPLE GET PROMOTED TO A POINT OF NO RETURN — SO KEEP THEM CHALLENGED

I have a short attention span and get bored easily. That is why I have enjoyed the mortgage business, where each and every client provides a set of unique challenges. By that same token, I always try and keep my team challenged by providing unique and interesting tasks for them to do.

TIP 3: FIND THE BLUE OCEAN AND SWIM IN IT (OR WORK SMARTER NOT HARDER)

A few years ago I was at a conference themed around the book *Blue Ocean Strategies*. I understood from that conference that what I had been doing for many years over numerous businesses is exactly that. I had never defined or refined it into any actual 'strategic terms', but we had always tried to find the blue ocean – unique ways of getting our business name out there and identifying differentiators in industries that are almost generic and commoditised.

TIP 4: PEOPLE, PEOPLE AND PEOPLE ARE CRITICAL TO ANY BUSINESS

In all my businesses, people and their interaction with the customers and fellow staff has been critical to the business success. I am considered 'soft' as a boss. I prefer to respect everyone and their own unique abilities and try to work with their strengths, whilst helping them grow and improve weaknesses.

TIP 5: HAVE A RELAXED OFFICE ENVIRONMENT

When interviewing new staff, I make the point that we will give them 'enough rope'[1] to either pull themselves out of the water or hang themselves. The office environments in all my businesses have been very relaxed, but have an underlying principle of ensuring that everyone pulls their weight. There is nowhere to hide in a small business.

TIP 6: HAVE A SERIOUS OFFICE CULTURE

A relaxed and serious office culture can exist in tandem. This can be achieved if the staff recognise that underlying the relaxed office culture is a very serious business that deals with people's lives and livelihood. Many organisations that I deal with focus too much on the seriousness of the work they do. They don't spend enough time ensuring that the workplace environment is warm and relaxed. It is a fine line for everyone to tread, but when it works, it works well.

TIP 7: COMMUNICATION IS KING. LONG LIVE THE KING

'Telling someone to go to hell in such a way that they look forward to the trip' was my late father's definition of diplomacy. I have positioned my mortgage businesses on a fundamental principal of communication. Over the years, when I have received complaints from clients, it has generally been around communication or lack

---

1   This line comes from an ABC network show in Australia, hosted by Andrew Denton called Enough Rope.

thereof. Almost daily, I stress to my team that communication with clients, even if it is one line that says, 'I checked on your file and the bank will give us an answer next Tuesday' makes the client feel part of the process. It makes the clients feel that their interests are being looked after. This makes our clients feel acknowledged that they are 'people' and not just 'files'.

TIP 8: GIVE UP CONTROL TO GAIN CONTROL

One of the key drivers for growth in my businesses is that I gave up control. I gave up control over the day-to-day grind of lodging and managing deals with the banks. By doing so, I gained control of my time to optimise my skills and do what I do best, which is being front-facing to new customers.

TIP 9: THE WHOLE TRUTH AND NOTHING BUT THE TRUTH

As simple as it sounds, being truthful all the time in dealing with everybody is a challenge. Often we slip into the all-too-easy trap of stretching the truth, like shifting blame to others. This links closely with the key focus of regular communication. If we communicate and everyone knows what is happening, then the truth is self-evident.

TIP 10: KEEP IT SIMPLE – IF ITS BITE-SIZE YOU CAN'T CHOKE

We tend to overcomplicate things. I see people who suffer from 'analysis paralysis' – analysing to a point where it is too hard to make any decisions. I absolutely believe in explaining structures and strategies to clients in simple terms that they can understand and terms that can easily be communicated to my team. This keep-it-simple approach has led to the development of a very simple but effective management system called 'Monday to Friday'. (More on this later)

TRAPS

The traps make the most sense in the context of stories and incidents and are part of the detail of the book.

Across the board, the key trap is that we, and members of our team, often forget why we are in business. I see people falling into this trap on a daily basis. Team members see their roles as quite specific in the organisation and focus on a specific role. They forget that everyone in the team is working towards a common goal of generating business and ultimately making a profit. It does not matter what part of the organisation a person represents; the common goal needs to be sustainability and profitability. Ultimately, business is about sales (see Chapter Five)

CHAPTER 3

BOTTOM(S) UP CULTURE

This chapter broadly looks at the elements that make up a corporate culture:

- What is culture?
- What drives culture?
- The cultural compass
- What are the mission and values of the culture?
- How do you plot a cultural course?

How can you govern a country which has 246 varieties of cheese?

CHARLES DE GAULLE

Success is a relative term. One person's success may be another's run of the mill. Each person defines success by their own standards and measures.

'When you look directly at an insane man all you see reflects your own knowledge that he's insane, which is not to see him at all. To see him you must see what he saw and when you are trying to see the vision of an insane man, an oblique route is the only way to come at it. Otherwise your own opinions block the way. There is

only one access to him that I can see as passable and we still have a way to go.[1]

How often do we look at someone's actions and flippantly say 'they are mad' when their actions don't reflect our reference point? How many times have you heard parents lament that their child is 'clever' but does not do well at exams? 'Exams are the worst system we know – but the best system we have'. Exams are a one-dimensional view of the measure of success. Not every child does well by that measure.

What's true for education is true for life. Not everybody can be measured on a one-dimensional scale. People who move to the beat of their own drum are often viewed as insane just because they are outside the norm. However, from their perspective, the normal position is shifted to a different normal.

The same can be said of organisational culture. Every organisation should define its own culture by its own cultural norms and standards. In an ideal world that is called the vision and mission of the organisation. In an ideal world, that is a shared vision and mission – shared with every member of the organisation. That same vision where every team member sees themselves as being part of a machine that delivers on the vision.

The key question is whether this ideal shared-vision organisation actually exists.

It may exist in the small, and even potentially the medium size sector of the business world. Growth often makes it impossible to manage the team alignment and commitment to a shared vision. The challenge for any organisation is to manage the growth in such a way that the culture and the commitment to the cultural values stays strong, no matter the scale or size.

---

1 This quote from Robert M Pirsig's *Zen and the Art of Motorcycle Maintenance* stuck with me.

CULTURE NEEDS TO BE A SHARED VISION

The first step for the leaders is to acknowledge that there may not be alignment of values and morals across the organisation. To manage that issue, my view, shared by several leading experts, is that cultural change must be driven from the bottom rather than being imposed from the top. This concept is gaining rapid momentum. There are many varietals of the idea that culture is what is done when the boss is away. *'Quality means doing it right when no one is looking. And culture means doing the right thing when no one is looking.'*[2]

The traditional approaches to developing corporate culture are dead. No longer is it the domain of management to decide on a vision and mission and blindly go about implementing that vision. The hope is that the employees will buy into the vision and mission and thereby shape an appropriate culture. But that is all that it is – a hope.

The traditional pyramid view allows the organisation to rest on a wide base of disparate views. The traditional wide base assumes that the disparate views provide a solid base for the organisation. I challenge this view.

I believe that the organisation needs to ensure that it rests on a bottom(s) up culture where the inverted pinnacle of the culture rests on a set of common shared values.

True corporate cultural renaissance comes from this inverted pyramid, with three levels:

THE BALANCING POINT

At the bottom of the pyramid sits the real actions of the team. This is the 'what happens'. Although this is the smallest point of the

---

2 Attributed to Henry Ford

inverted pyramid it is probably the most critical. The rest of the organisation sits on this singular point.

It means that the management need to understand the actions of the team at a grass roots level. Questions that need to be asked to give management an understanding of the organisation include:

- What do the team do?
- What do the individuals do when left to their own devices?
- What actions do the team members individually and collectively take in response to certain inputs?

Management need to employ techniques and strategies to understand these core cultural attributes of the team.

The team culture in the mortgage business is one of a commitment to a collective vision. The vision is not actually defined on a laminated wall chart. It does however encompass a vision where success is measured in clients' eyes as achieving the clients desired outcome whilst recognising that staff are our most valuable asset.

THE MIDDLE BIT

The middle bit of the pyramid is the meat of the organisation. It is the set of rules that defines the relationship between the actual operational culture and the vision and mission. It is the somewhat boring but extremely necessary set of rules, policies and procedures that define the boundaries of how things are done. This defines the organisational culture on a far clearer level than vision and mission statements.

THE TOP BIT

At the top end of the inverted pyramid is the traditional mission and values of the organisation. However, it is dependent on being aligned with the small point at the bottom of the inversion. The mission and values are truly dependent on the leadership and their understanding of the team, the team values and the team's understanding of the corporate mission.

A Bottom's Up Culture

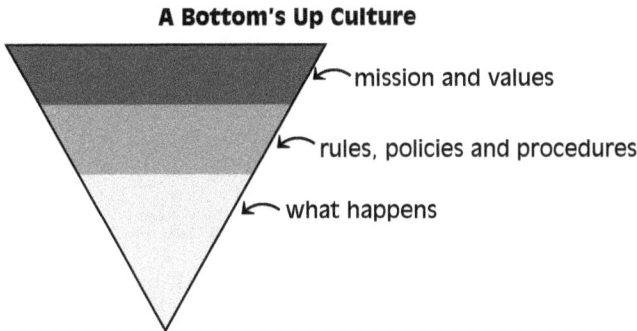

mission and values

rules, policies and procedures

what happens

The first step in changing the culture or potentially realigning it is for management to understand 'how things actually get done'. Then they can assess how to apply it to accelerate and drive the cultural shift.

Tools that management and leadership need to use to understand the culture of what actually happens:

THE CULTURAL COMPASS

The compass is the most basic of navigation tools, yet it has saved the lives of countless people. The compass has a needle that always points in a specific direction – magnetic north. You could say that the needle is attracted to that direction and almost 'wants' to move in that direction.

When I got my private pilot's license, we were educated on the difference between true north and magnetic north. If you don't know which one to use when navigating or which north your equipment is showing, then you could lose your way quickly. The difference between true north and magnetic north varies between places in the world. So, each place on earth has a different relationship between true north and magnetic north. In much the same vein, every country and culture operate on a different moral compass.

The compass-analogy can be applied to various aspects of organisational life and culture and provides some direction in looking at:

- Employees moral compass as applied individually
- Team compass providing direction
- Varied directions taken by corporate silos
- Accepted societal norms of various locations

What moral compass are the employees using?

UNDERSTAND THE DIRECTION YOU ARE HEADING

We would all like to believe that the moral compass of the organisation is perfectly aligned with that of the team. The fact is that they rarely are.

'To err is human – to blame the other person is more human.'[3]

I had the experience of doing some work with an organisation with just this problem. The culture of the organisation was and unfortunately still is to 'blame someone else'. Whenever it was clear that the team had made an error, no-one stepped up and took responsibility. The blame game started at the slightest hint of an issue. The core cultural problem is that this started with the leadership who shirked responsibility and always found ways

---

3 Humorous twist on the original words of Shakespeare.

to duck and dive around a problem without ever admitting some form of liability.

The role of the leader is to step up and face responsibility even if they do not have a direct responsibility for the issue. The concept of a leader 'falling on his sword' is incredibly powerful. True leaders will accept that the actions of the team are collectively reflective of their own performance.

THE TRUTH — AND NOTHING BUT

There are times when the leader does need to apportion blame in order to move forward. When it is exceedingly evident that a person on the team 'messed up' the good leaders should be looking at the larger picture of the mistake. It is important to ascertain whether the mistake was deliberate or a true mistake. In the latter case, leaders can manage the process of containing the fallout. A weak manager will blame the person who made the mistake – irrespective of whether they could have done otherwise or not. A strong manager will, especially in the case of a true mistake, find ways to improve employee performance in the future to avoid the mistake.

In the case of a deliberate error, whether by omission or action, true leaders will not be afraid to execute the necessary steps to remedy the action and ensure that it does not happen again. This may mean managing the performance of the employee to a point of resignation or termination.

One of my core philosophies has been to make sure that I am always dealing with 'the truth and the whole truth'.

In the mortgage business when faced with making a hard call to a client, I have taken the opportunity to use the call to move forward. (A hard call is generally one with unwelcome news). The first is to tell the truth. The second is to try to find some good news, or at least, a productive way forward, for example, 'this lender may have declined your loan, but we have another alternative ....

I personally make those calls from the open plan area, amidst the staff. The staff see and hear that I am not afraid to make the call and, more importantly, they learn how to make the calls and deal with clients.

Over the years the staff have drifted towards making the calls themselves as they feel empowered and knowledgeable enough to do so with confidence.

ETHICS DEFINE THE MORAL COMPASS

A few years ago, I had to terminate the contract of a sub-contract broker on the team.

At the time there was a disparity in the commission structures paid by various lenders. This was problematic from a management perspective as often the lenders paying us the most commission were building that commission into the rate and not offering the best deal to our client. Some of these lenders had niche products that were applied specifically to certain clients and fulfilled a need. These clients were and still are more concerned about getting the deal done rather than the best rate, and so in these cases, the 'lowest rate' is not the deciding factor.

I had implemented a compliance form, where the team member who chose a product for a client would have to write a paragraph on the file notes about why he (or she) chose that product.

This broker wrote in his file notes that his choice of lender was driven by being paid the higher commission – an unacceptable answer in my eyes – hence the termination.

Similarly, was a lender who approached me to have a presentation to the team around their products. As normal, when the lender arrived, I asked him to tell me in 30 seconds, why we should use his products. His answer was that they paid the 'highest commission in the industry'. I politely asked him to leave as I did not want to tempt my team into choosing the wrong lender based on remuneration.

In the main, a good salesman can upsell any product, but in the mortgage space where brokers are giving advice and are seen (hopefully) as trusted advisers, this poses a challenge. A consumer is looking to the broker to give the right advice – the advice that is right for their unique situation. They believe that the advice is the 'best product for them'. I felt, and still feel that it is immoral to tempt the team members towards a product based on their remuneration rather than the client interests.

So how does this apply to the moral compass? I believe that as a leader, I have created an environment in each of my businesses where the commitment to clients, through honesty and integrity, are at the forefront. This has helped align the moral compass of the team members with the corporate morality.

There is no doubt that when management follow a process of finding out what is done and how it is done in the organisation – they will come across many aspects of corporate behaviour that conflict with the preferred actions. The challenge then becomes how you steer the ship to get alignment and direction. How do you move magnetic north to a point where everyone is comfortable with the compass pointing in that direction? Conversely, how do you manage those employees that resist the alignment of their direction with that of the organisation?

The first step in the process is to understand the 'what is done'. A process of anonymous consultation is useful, where employees can express their views, where employees can explain the 'what is done' in the times when the boss is away.

The next step in the navigation process is ensuring that the chart or map is the correct one. It would be challenging trying to navigate a certain course when it's not even on the map. When I had a private pilot licence we relied heavily on charts as GPS technology was not readily available. Each area was broken down into many sub-sections and to have enough detail on the charts, you would sometimes need to chart your course over multiple maps. Fundamentally, this is no different to the corporation. Each department or team may have a completely different culture and focus. It would be expected that the engineers are most likely to have a completely different culture to the marketing team.

Often departments in the same organisation have distinctly varied cultures and by extension mission and values.

I believe that you now understand the problem and the challenge. The problem is ensuring that all parts of the organisation are operating on the same chart. With the right tools and research, you can now have an understanding of 'how things are done' in your organisation.

Once you establish the direction that the culture in the organisation should be taking, you can plot a course to get there. This may sound like old school strategy development: Management sets up a vision and mission strongly encouraging the team to follow that direction. This is not what I am advocating. I am advocating an ideal utopian world where the team, in all business areas, is committed to the fundamental value system of the organisation. Where each team understands their role in the organisation and aims to get the best from their team to achieve the common organisational goal. The fundamental understanding is that the overall vision and mission is still largely directed by the leadership team. It must be flexible enough to move and shift towards a space between the leadership vision and the team actions.

Is that achievable? I believe it is – with the disclaimer that utopia is not. But that does not stop us from striving for utopia.

So first, a compass is a fundamental tool in working out the direction that the staff are taking and using it to develop a corporate culture. The next step is using the same compass and plotting the course of the company. The company culture is most likely determined by the staff and their actions. The aim is for the corporate culture to be stronger than the individuals and become 'a badge of honour' to be passed on.

I challenge business leaders to have the courage to ask basic questions such as:

- Describe the company values in your own words

- The company values are ...

- The company supports me by ...

The responses to these and many more questions will allow management to gain an understanding of the culture and values of the team. Leaders and managers then need to have the courage and foresight to place their expected vision, mission and values alongside the actual values and culture of the team. When these don't align, the challenge is to delve deeper into trying to under-stand the misalignment.

All team members need to work towards finding the correct solution. One quirky comment I heard many years ago was a manager imploring the team to get their ducks in a row. One team member suggested that that would be ok if they 'quacked in sequence'.

NEVER ASK YOUR TEAM TO DO ANYTHING YOU WOULD NOT DO

The philosophy of the boss 'providing the vision – it's your job to implement it' is partly correct. It is the job of managers and leaders to work out the vision and mission of the organisation. However, it is their job to implement it, or at least be a critical element. Implementation of the vision and mission needs to be a bottom(s) up approach where the culture of the organisation is driven from all sides and brings together everyone to a shared vision and mission. It comes back to 'never ask staff to do anything you would not do'.

I am sure that many bosses believe that they subscribe to this philosophy, however I would contend that many people see their promotion in the corporation as a chance to no longer do the work.

CHALLENGE THE TEAM

Better managers understand that although they may no longer do certain tasks, the fact that they can do the tasks should provide opportunities to help team members grow and develop.

Analogy: A goldfish is swimming in a bowl. Every time he passes the fake rock he says, 'hey wow – there is a rock'.

As a manager and leader one of the greatest challenges is to keep your team challenged and motivated. The fine balance between delegating tasks and empowering the team is also one of keeping the team challenged. Always assume that the team need as many challenges as you do.

A seemingly overlooked, but as important aspect, is the alignment of all silos within the organisation. Each silo needs to see themselves as a contributor to the success of the organisation.

As corporations grow, they develop these silos, where each silo loses focus on the core business.

I challenge you as a manager and leader to look at the organisation with new eyes. I challenge you to look at the culture and consider whether the alignment of the mission and values is truly what you want.

CHAPTER 4

GIVE UP CONTROL
TO GAIN CONTROL

Early on I realised that I had to hire people smarter and more qualified than I was in a number of different fields, and I had to let go of a lot of decision-making. I can't tell you how hard that is. But if you've imprinted your values on the people around you, you can dare to trust them to make the right moves.

HOWARD SCHULTZ

I am often asked by finance brokers to explain how I managed to grow the mortgage business quickly.

The answer: I gave up control over the day-to-day grind of lodging and managing deals with the banks. By doing so, I gained control of my time to optimise it and do what I do best, which is being front facing to new customers. In corporate terms, that would be called New Business Development.

The barrier for most brokers in the early 2000s was the lack of scalability. We, like many others in the industry, believed that the key to growing the business was centred around employing many brokers. At one stage, we had 18 brokers and no support staff. My partner and I were seeing clients, collating paperwork, submitting to the banks and doing all the follow up. The turning point was realising that employing and empowering staff around us would enable the business to grow .

It was also originally one of the motivations for writing this book.

Giving up control to gain control is the result of the process of taking a business through the pains that allow it to grow.

To give up control you need a team. I am a firm believer in the concept of a team. It's incredibly hard to be an island. Human nature dictates that survival chances are so much higher in a group. This chapter deals with:

- Why do I play sport as a pretty average sportsman?

- Why is a team approach important?

- How are leaders part of teams?

- Leaders need to be followers.

- Giving up control to gain control.

- How the team and I become one.

- The importance of empowerment in the team.

- Conveying the team approach to clients.

In the early days at high school, we were offered the choice between rugby and hockey. I had braces on my teeth, so I was told that hockey would be my choice. By the second year of high school, I realised that I had some talent for the game, not star quality but as a consistent team player. I joined a club outside the school and by the third year at high school I was playing for the first team of the school and regular Sunday club games at senior level.

One of the challenges at school was defending our sport against the 'men's men' in the rugby team. Rugby was the premier sport in South Africa, somewhat akin to a national religion. Being a minority taught resilience and the ability to stand up for what I believed in.

I continued playing hockey for a few years after school. When I started work at Vaal Reefs Gold Mine, I was lucky enough to be selected for the Western Transvaal (State) Under-21 indoor hockey side. The same year (1986) I was also selected for the Western Trans-vaal Senior side to play in the South African Country Districts. I was never the star player in any team, merely a team member.

LEADING BY FOLLOWING

Years later I took up an interest in cycling. I heard and learned the term 'domestique', used to refer to the team players or 'sloggers' who carried and assisted the team star.

José Luis Arrieta was a domestique for Miguel Indurain. *L'Équipe* newspaper said: 'He no longer counts the hours, the years, spent with his nose in the wind trying to protect his leader for as long as possible'.

Arrieta summed up his career by saying, 'When you have the chance to start your career in so big a team and at the side of a champion as great as Indurain, you grow in the service of sacrifice. I don't complain. To the contrary, I had the chance to live some wonderful moments. When Indurain won, or another rider for whom we had decided to work, it was a victory for all the team men as well.'

How does someone who is an innately A type personality, learn to be part of a team, and listen to others within that team and the team leader? It took me years to stop listening to my own voice and listen to others. However, in the team sense, particularly in hockey, I had a complete personality transformation. I realised that I was a small cog in the team, and that my role, albeit narrowly defined was a crucial element of the team. I stopped playing hockey in early 1989 and resumed in 2015. In the interim period, every sport I did was individual, whether running, cycling, golf or triathlon. It was quite exhilarating to suddenly play team sport again, albeit at over-50 Masters level, and be part of the team.

The lesson is that sometimes a leader needs to learn to follow.

≈≈≈

There was a joke once told about the US president questioning the Israeli president on their leadership challenges. The US President said that he did not understand the problem in Israel as he was the leader of 300 million people. The Israeli President said - the problem arose from being the president of 6 million 'presidents'.

ALIGN PERSONAL AND TEAM GOALS

The biggest challenge as a team member is understanding your individual role in the team. There are many stories and analogies about how teams are like an engine. The team will function when all the parts are moving correctly and each one is doing what it was designed to do. But a trivial, tiny part – say one tooth on the smallest cog in the machine that is not functioning will cause the entire engine to fail.

Sometimes in business it is not too critical if the pieces don't exactly fit, but when they do all fit, it is remarkable to see how all these small elements meld together to make a highly-tuned working machine.

As a junior engineer at Vaal Reefs Gold Mine, one of my greatest challenges was understanding my role within the organisation. As a young university engineering graduate, I believed the world was my oyster. This, coupled with an intrinsic belief in my own ability, caused a daily questioning of my role. I had an inherent understanding of the operational aspects of the mining operation, and the broad role of the engineer and the engineering team. As a junior engineer, we were tasked with quite specific, narrowly defined areas of responsibility. Possibly the arrogance of youth and the desire to climb the ladder quickly drove my desire to see the big picture. I could not understand my fellow engineers who were happy with their limited tasks and responsibility. They focused on the next level on the ladder where I was probably focused on what were the responsibilities and tasks many levels up.

In December 1996, the three engineers on the mine shaft where I was working (I was the 4th and most junior) decided to all take leave simultaneously and left me in charge. This was an incredible opportunity for a 22-year-old engineer to be in control and have some real responsibility. There were two major learning experiences from that. The first – a positive – was that most of the team, especially the black workers called me 'Makosi' which is 'little boss'. Many years later I understood that it was a term of endearment reserved for a boss of small stature (I am only 1.67 m tall) that was used to convey respect. On reflection, it was quite a compliment for a white kid from Johannesburg to earn the title 'Makosi'.

When I resigned from Anglo American to go to business school, my farewell card said 'when you come back to take over Anglo American, please remember us'. I only really understood this comment over the passage of time and finally took it as a cue to sometimes wind back the enthusiasm and ambition. I am often quoted as saying, 'I wish I had more energy or less ambition.'

30

GIVE UP CONTROL

You cannot build a successful team until you empower the team members. This requires a level of trust that goes far beyond a book of rules. It requires the leader of the team to give up control. This does not mean letting team members do their own thing. It means giving up control and allowing team members to work to their potential.

The second key learning was somewhat negative, but contributed to shaping my view of an effective work team. I noticed that every manager and employee was scrutinised from all sides. This led to most managers creating silos where they were the centre of everything that happened and there was no delegation, devolution of responsibility or effective cross-working. The managers were far more concerned about other people having the ability to do the manager's job than the greater picture of creating an enabled workforce. This made me realise that the large corporation was not for me, and more importantly that I would develop a completely different culture in any venture that I undertook.

In my mortgage businesses, I have taken the team to the next level. The team members introduce themselves to the client and are given the responsibility of managing the client from application to settlement. I expect that they will take the client to heart. Recently, one of the team came to me and said that she had been up since 4.30 am worrying about a particular client file. My response was 'welcome to my world'.

Keep away from people who try to belittle your ambitions. Small people always do that, but the really great make you feel that you, too, can become great.

– MARK TWAIN

When we first employed assistants in the mortgage business it allowed Jon and I to gain control of our time by releasing control of the process to a member of the team. You cannot force an employee to embrace the clients and culture with the same vigour as the entrepreneur. However, the extent to which they have embraced the culture and taken control of the process is a good measure of success. It is also significantly a measure of the differentiation of the business. If we as a team don't exhibit passion and caring for the clients, then we are no different to the business or bank down the road where clients are merely a number. Over the years I have regularly been faced by the team members' own feelings as they take each failure personally and each success as one for the team.

BE PREPARED TO STAND OUT AND BE PART OF THE TEAM

A business school is the place to find a hundred presidents. But the business school structure of working in syndicates counters that. Here six to eight students (mostly Type-A personalities) were grouped into syndicates which are not unlike project teams pulled together in the corporate world. The syndicates were responsible for delivering at least half of the work which contributed to the syndicate member's final results.

The syndicate approach is an interesting experiment in social interaction and management. Taking a number of leaders and putting them in an environment where teamwork and cooperation are vital is a challenge. Another aspect is the trust that each of us needed to believe enough in the other syndicate members and their ability to represent us as a group.

The lesson for me at the age of 25, at business school (where I believed I was invincible) was that learning to be a part of the team and empowering someone else to be a leader can be very rewarding.

In retrospect, I probably did not do that well. I probably did not allow the other team members the courtesy of my full attention and got irritated when they did not follow my ideas. I hope that I have developed more tolerance and understanding over time.

An essential part of a team is recognising the individuals within a team, and those that are happy to stand up for themselves as well. The team needs to have common goals and objectives, but relies heavily on individuals' commitment to the team goals.

In the opening scene of the movie 'Life of Brian' (1979 – Monty Python) many disciples gather on the mountain listening to the 'Messiah'. The Messiah shouts 'we are all individuals' to which the entire crowd on the mountain responds 'we are all individuals'. One lone voice says, 'no, I'm not'. I believe that lone voice should be a team member, empowered enough to stand out, but also with an understanding of their role in the team.

In growing a business, particularly an entrepreneurial business, the founder(s) or entrepreneurs need to employ staff at some point, but in all my business ventures, we were most certainly hands-on for a large part of the startup and growth phases. I don't believe a business can be successful without the driving forces understanding the detail that makes up all aspects of the business. It is impossible to develop and improve business processes without the necessary understanding of how the system works and its flaws.

NEVER ASK STAFF TO DO ANYTHING YOU WOULD NOT DO. BUT THEN LET THEM DO IT.

In the early days of the education business, both Jon and I were intimately involved in every aspect of the business. It allowed us to work out better ways of doing things so that when we employed staff to do those tasks we could train them in the best possible way.

One of the most fundamental aspects of employing staff is empowerment – giving them some of the responsibility for some business tasks. It is also important to recognise that the passion and commitment shown by the entrepreneurs will most likely not be exhibited by staff. This does not mean that the staff are not loyal or committed to the vision of the business, but 'the buck does not stop' with them. The entrepreneurs still have ultimate control of the business, and ultimate passion for it. Part of the skill of growing a business and employing staff is the motivation of those staff to buy into the team and the organisation.

One of the most critical times in the evolution of the mortgage business was when I employed my first processor (or PA). His role was to do the paperwork as my back office. Up until that point, we (Jon and I) believed that the growth of the business would be by employing more brokers and at one stage, had 18 brokers on the team, but no support staff. Employing a support person was almost an epiphany in the business. It allowed me to see that a smaller number of good talented brokers, backed by a strong support team would do wonders and be far more productive than a team of brokers with no support. Over the years, I have advised many brokers to 'give up control to gain control'. The simple idea around this is that the professional can be far more productive with support.

When recruiting new brokers to the industry, I insist that they process all of their own deals from start to finish, with our assistance and guidance. The rationale is that if they have not done each of these tasks in the process, and done them well, then it will be near impossible for them to get a PA to do them efficiently or understand if the PA is being efficient.

In the mortgage business, each transaction is different. Therefore, the training of staff faced some unique challenges. In many organisations, staff can be trained to a specific set of processes. When the nature of each transaction changes, in an environment that is very heavily transaction and process based, it brings some degree of difficulty. Over the years, we have evolved methods of training new admin staff that encompass the rote process initially and then a gradual shift to the more complex lending.

However herein lies the fundamental challenge for most brokers in my industry. Finance and mortgage broking is by its very nature a detail driven process. Therefore, most brokers would like to be in control and struggle to trust anyone to do the job as well as they could. This leads to micromanagement and, in fact, probably a loss of productivity in the short term, whilst the staff member is being trained. Each unique detail for each case offers a challenge for learning, and prevents boredom.

'In this organisation we give you enough rope – it's up to you to pull yourself out of the water or drown'. The key driver of setting up a successful back office is the idea of being able to 'give up control'. As soon as you are confident that the staff member (or file driver as they are called) can drive the back office process, then you 'gain control'. You gain control of your time and can direct your time to productive activities – like seeing clients or business development.

The processes I have set up and the protocols and communication lines ensure that I don't lose control entirely. I make a point of sitting in the open plan office with the team a few times a week and spending some time with each team member being updated on the progress of all the files on which they are working. This allows me to be back in control and make decisions, without the weight of the 'processing' slowing me down.

I am at pains to explain the process to clients. I explain that I'm not dumping them, but that they now have two contact people – one for fundamental daily processing issues and myself for strategic issues. This is usually after a meeting of an hour or more with them. I explain that without my team, my processing engine,

I would not have been able to spend personal and personalised time with them. The team approach allows me to be freed up to do what I do best, which is meeting and working out a strategy for clients.

CHAPTER 5

BUSINESS IS ABOUT SALES
(DON'T TELL THE MARKETING GURUS)

Management is, above all, a practice where art, science and craft meet.

HENRY MINTZBERG

Marketing definitely has a place. There is the old idea that if you build a better mousetrap the people won't come and buy it until you tell them about it. However, it does not always have to be big and bold. Not every company has the budget to look at big picture marketing. It can be small and subtle.

Marketing gurus have created an aura around the marketing fundamentals. But this chapter will cover the fundamental *business* ideas around understanding that all business ultimately relies on revenue which is a direct function of sales. These include:

- Finding new ways to market business that may seem somewhat commoditised.

- Everyone is a salesman – some are just better than others (and what makes them better).

- Everyone is involved in marketing; it's not done in isolation.

- Small businesses tend to blur the sales/marketing divide better than corporations.

- Small business needs to find niche areas to compete and differentiate.

Find the blue ocean and swim in it, but be confident enough to spend time swimming in the red ocean.

A few years ago, I attended a mortgage conference themed around the book *Blue Ocean Strategy* by W Chan Kim and Renée Mauborgne. The subtitle of the book is 'creating uncontested market space'. I believe that our businesses have in many ways managed to find the blue ocean, if not in its entirety, but finding enough space to swim in water that is not overcrowded.

When I got to understand the concepts discussed in the 'blue ocean strategies' I realised that, although we had been looking for the blue ocean and uncontested market space in many ways, we still needed to compete in what is known as the red ocean. The red ocean is the overcrowded generic market place where there is little or no differentiation between business offerings.

Triathlons and swimming in competitive open water 'races' taught me the difference between the blue and red oceans. The blue ocean was the calm water around the periphery of the main body of swimmers where you could swim in relative peace without being kicked in the head by the swimmers ahead of you and without kicking those behind you. The red ocean was the 'washing machine' in the middle of the pack where you are battered from all sides and limited by the movement of the general pack.

Further analysis of the ideas around the blue ocean, reveal that one cannot always change an entire business to operate in the blue ocean. Sometimes we need to change just small aspects of the business.

In looking at this, I decided to combine a number of ideas to see if I could construct a new model that reflected the business from my perspective. One idea that I learned at business school was a concept called functional benchmarking. You break your business down into various operational slices. Then you benchmark each slice against the leader in that field (often well outside your own industry), rather than trying to benchmark the whole business. An example that was commonly used (in the late 1980s) was in the case of a company trying to find the best billing system for their business. They should have compared their system to what was regarded as the best at the time, being American Express and then modelled their 'slice' of their business on that specific leader, even if their business was not remotely connected to American Express.

Bringing these two concepts together – the Blue Ocean and the Functional Benchmark – I call finding the *functional blue ocean*. There are many marketing gurus who delve into the ideas around niche markets and marketing. This is more than that. It is about dissecting the business into a myriad of components, perhaps even along non-traditional lines, and then looking to see where each of those areas can improve and find its blue ocean.

Finding uncontested market space is finding space to operate in which there is little competition. In some of the business ventures I have been involved in, our niche became our ability to adapt and adapt quickly to changing conditions.

When we started our business in South Africa my partner Jon and I were young MBA graduates who thought we could teach the world how to run their businesses. This was essentially what we saw as our blue ocean.

We started a business called Innovative Management Development (IMD). Jon, with the help of his wife Lara, worked out a logo that incorporated interesting designs – a chess piece for strategy, a world for globalisation and a book for knowledge. The Latin saying *'quo sapientior eo ditior'* – 'Profiting business through knowledge' formed the bottom of the crest.

PROFITING BUSINESS THROUGH KNOWLEDGE

In retrospect, the focus on logo and slogan was pretentious and naive. It could probably have had any name and achieved equal success. I often see people today who spend days and weeks fretting about the name and corporate logo for a new business. Equally we see large corporates go through strategic rebranding every few years. In recent times, company names and their ability to link to reliable website addresses become more critical than the actual names and corporate image. In fact, the corporate image is most likely portrayed through the web page today.

Our focus at IMD was on creating the illusion of size, scale and professionalism. One of our most important aspects of the business was that we understood the need to look more established than we

40

were. So, we contacted a few friends who we knew had been at various business schools. They agreed to lend us their 'names' for the business. We went out marketing our services looking like a group of 10 MBA Graduates. By design we managed to incorporate graduates from 3 local business schools and 2 internationals schools. We were competing for business against many larger more experienced consulting firms. Despite having the million-dollar look we were quite thin on the ground financially and were pretty much running on fumes. This led to the necessity to be overly clever in finding niches in whatever we did to preserve the little cash resources we had.

We need to go back a few steps to understand the rationale for starting IMD. When I did my final MBA research project it was entitled 'Management Development Requirements in a Changing South Africa'. As part of the research I sent questionnaires to the top 100 listed companies in South Africa. They were surveyed on plans and strategies in human resource development.

We started IMD (as a consultancy) by using the MBA research as a hook to contact companies to engage with us. Reporting the findings was in fact making a pitch for IMD to get consulting training work from them. When we did that pitch it was based on scale, scope and professionalism, or so we believed.

We developed, with Jon's brother in law, Wayne, a video presentation – a kind of very early PowerPoint. With Wayne we made and developed a 35mm slide presentation, then projected it onto a screen whilst Wayne did the voice over. This was shot to a VHS Video tape using a home video camera. It was very professional at the time, but in the current age of PowerPoint and Prezi, it was very amateurish.

We then purchased a small TV with a built-in video player and lugged that around to all these corporate offices showing our presentation. It was literally lugged around, it weighed more than 25kg and was in a transport box around 80cm^2 and 1m high. The only way to move it long distances was on an industrial trolley. In retrospect it must have been quite funny to watch these two guys in suits, trying to look slick and professional, dragging a big blue suitcase on a trolley into corporate headquarters in Johannesburg.

ALWAYS BELIEVE IN YOURSELF

Our (then) slick approach and professionalism was ahead of most others, and proved that you did not need the $1000 suits, but you did need an absolute belief in self. Jon and I came into these meetings as young MBAs with a pitch and story well beyond our age and stage in life. We delivered it with confidence and never for one minute believed that we would oversell and underdeliver.

We managed to win a contract with Eskom (Electricity Supply Commission of South Africa) to develop and deliver 'quality management programmes', something we knew nothing about. However, as I will refer to many times, the MBA gave us small amounts of knowledge about a variety of topics, and equipped us with the skill and knowledge to research a topic, and in a short space of time, sound like an expert. Eskom agreed to fly us to a few remote power stations to do research on their quality management and systems. We then developed the first module of a series of ten, each priced at R17 000 (at the time that was around $10 000 Aud), a lot of money in those days.

One of the contractual conditions was that after the development of each module, we had to present a training course to a large group of employees. We 'hired' one of our friends to be present to add numbers when we presented the first module of the programme. We thought it was quite successful and well-received. However, in every blue ocean there are always a few sharks. It was at that point that Eskom contracted a large international consulting firm that offered them significant cost savings by analysing the business and suggesting areas where Eskom could rationalise.

UNDERSTAND YOUR TARGET

One of the first suggestions from these consultants was to cancel all contracts with their other 'consultants'. We got paid but had no paying work in the pipeline. In retrospect, we learned that despite our appearance of size and depth of knowledge we did not understand the fundamental drivers of monolithic government bodies, especially regarding employee motivation and the natural instinct of people to preserve their jobs and their 'empires'. Although the ideas around quality management were leading edge, no-one was prepared to take responsibility and be seen as a cost centre in an era where the corporate philosophy was about drastic cost saving measures.

One of the key learning aspects of that period was about Chutzpah – a Yiddish word for cheek – although meaning more than that. It proved that with a bit of chutzpah, you can go far. I guess that in some way we created some blue ocean and went for a swim. That swim was short-lived, but enjoyable and taught us a lot.

After Eskom terminated the contract, we were at a loss as to what to do. My wife Rafaella was working, earning around R1100 per month as a teacher. We contacted the Institute of Marketing Management (IMM) to see if we could become accredited marketing consultants.

DON'T OVER-ANALYSE

The IMM suggested that we start a school and teach our (IMM's) diploma course. That was in late 1990 and we had nothing to lose – we had no work anyway. We had the perfect combination of factors that would normally scream 'don't do it'. We had limited money for advertising and had no premises, classrooms or teachers. We set up an office at Jon's house designed some advertising and started advertising courses to start in 1991. Those early days of being an entrepreneur were critical to the formation of many of my business philosophies. Many of the tips and traps were formed in those days.

We found a 'law school' where students could attend night classes while studying for the admission exam for registration as a lawyer. Their facilities were unused during the day, so we agreed to rent them daily for a nominal amount. We also decided to run some part-time lectures and needed space in the evenings. At the time we managed to convince the technical college in Johannesburg to lease us one classroom in the evenings.

In funding terms, we were vastly undercapitalised. We did little market analysis. If we did, we would have discovered two large players dominating that space and a few well-established niche players. The private education market in South Africa in 1990 was somewhat mature. But in retrospect, if we had done some detailed business analysis around the changes in Africa, the release of Nelson Mandela and the unbanning of the African National Congress, we would probably have realised that there was a need and hunger for education amongst the mostly uneducated mass of people in South Africa. This coincidence of timing and the fact that we were always willing to try innovative marketing techniques probably combined and created our niche.

We designed a few adverts that spoke about our brilliant team of lecturers, ran them in the newspapers and hoped for the best. Jon always made the joke 'what happens if we throw a party and everyone comes'. We had one phone line (at Jon's house) and we sat there for weeks answering the calls with a 'professional' approach, as if we had been doing it for years.

To this day, we are amazed that we managed to convince around 20 students to sign up for day classes and an equivalent number for night classes. We spent our days at the computer (we had only one) typing notes for students. Then stood at the copier making copies ready for the evening classes. The tip 'I will never ask the staff to do a task that I would not do' stems back to these early days of IMD. When registration days were held our wives and other family members pitched in to help so that prospective students saw a much bigger team. Given that we did not have permanent premises, Jon and I were seen many times carrying our one and only overhead slide projector from our cars to our lectures and then back home again.

Besides, for one course in Business Communications we ensured that Jon and I could lecture and deliver any course on offer. There were two reasons. One, we needed the money, and two, we never wanted to be beholden to anyone.

By the middle of 1991, this was starting to look like a bona fide business, so we took the next plunge of finding permanent premises. We found premises across the road from the University of the Witwatersrand (Wits). The premises were a one-floor walkup, upstairs from a second-hand golf equipment shop. This was our home for a few years. The culture we developed in those days was relaxed. When Jon and I felt like a break from the office we would go down the back steps of the building, into the basement storeroom of the golf shop and spend time hitting balls into the practice net.

The accidental design of where the college was located became a major selling point for potential students. Our marketing pitch was that although they, the students, were not university students they would be 'in the university precinct' and gain the benefits of student life. Additionally, we employed a few university lecturers to deliver our courses, so the students were getting the 'very same' lecturers as the campus across the road.

In 1993 we started our second college in Durban, around a six-hour drive from Johannesburg. Suddenly we needed to create systems and strategies for remotely managing a campus a large distance away – a good exercise in control.

We found premises, hired some staff and started running some advertising. We used whatever technology was available to us at the time. One of those was the ability to divert calls to another number. So, we got a number in Durban and diverted it to Johannesburg to the head office. To track the calls, we used an alias starting with the letter D. Then when potential students called the number it was transparent and they thought they were talking to a local person in Durban.

POSITIONING

When I started in the Mortgage industry, the norm at the time was that mortgage brokers would do home visits. Once I had established an office and infrastructure I gradually began to suggest to clients that they should come into our offices to meet with myself or one of the team. Initially there was some resistance to this, in part driven by a large industry group advertising that their brokers would 'visit in the comfort of your own home'. I took the reverse approach and positioned ourselves as professional advisers and as such have said to many clients 'you don't expect your lawyer or accountant to visit at home'. Over the years, I have had less than a dozen clients refuse to come into the offices. I am absolutely committed to positioning of the mortgage broker as a true professional and hence the ideas around home visits.

TAKE YOURSELF SERIOUSLY

The second cultural aspect of the IMD colleges was the relaxed office environment counterbalanced by the very serious approach to students and their future. At the end of the day, our students wrote external exams which gave us a definite yardstick as to the success or failure of our business. On a micro level, it allowed us to have an external measure of the performance of every staff member. The review process was not formalised, but all lecturers worked to the best of their ability and the student's ability to achieve the best possible results. Lecturing staff were always measured and reemployed based on historical performance on external exams.

One of the key successes of the business was our willingness to try fresh marketing spaces. We realised early on that we did not have the marketing budget to match our well-funded larger competitors. The readiness to shoot from the hip gave us speed to market.

MARKETING ON A BUDGET CAN BE EXTREMELY EFFECTIVE

For the IMD education business, we looked for places to advertise for maximum exposure. We started advertising small black and white adverts in various sections of the papers (Business, News and Entertainment). Each advert carried a different name on the advert for the contact person so that we could monitor the source of the call. The adverts read 'call Debbie Now' or 'contact Susan to secure your place'.

In those days all TV in South Africa was free to air with limited channels. Most people would consult the TV guide daily for their entertainment. We approached the main paper in Johannesburg *(The Star)* and convinced them to sell us the advertising space under the TV guide. This was a full color page and was expensive space, but it allowed us the opportunity to look bigger than we were. It bought us a level of credibility. We created this **blue ocean** and it took around six months for our financially well-resourced competitors to respond and start bidding for the space that we had created. We then started to look for our next advertising niche as we had to keep searching for the next advantage over the larger competitors.

We started a similar advertising campaign in *The Sowetan* newspaper. This was a paper aimed at the majority black population in South Africa. Despite the unbanning of the African National Congress (ANC) and movement towards the first democratic elections the remnants of apartheid were still very much alive. In April 1994, around a month before the first democratic elections, we were invited to a traditional 'African celebration' at *The Sowetan*, held in Soweto[1]. We were one of a small group of mostly white advertisers invited to this event, and we began to realise that what we thought was a small advertising budget was quite large for *The Sowetan*. This was quite an accolade for two guys who started a few years earlier on a shoestring budget. The humorous aside to this story was that as all white guests were arriving were handed a printed set of the lyrics of Nkosi Sikelel' iAfrika which at the time was accepted by the majority of the population as the unofficial national anthem. The assumption was that the majority of the white guests would not know the words, which I would have to admit was indeed correct.

The main lesson was that we truly believed in our product and the delivery of it. We were happy to commit to adventurous advertising to get the students as we knew we would deliver. Much like when we started as a consultancy, we padded our 'team' in order to add to our credibility. That same credibility was on the line in the deliverable and we had absolute faith in our ability to deliver

1 Soweto – or South West Townships was an area designated by the apartheid governments of South Africa as an area in which people of colour should live. Apartheid meant separate development and the government enforced it through racially segregated areas. The Soweto uprising of 1976 was a major event towards the eventual dismantling of official apartheid in the 90s.

a top-level service and programme. The same advertising strategy was applied in all the cities that we opened offices. From 1992 to 1995 we opened five additional offices around South Africa. The strategy worked for a relatively extended period until our larger competitors found the space and started to outspend us. Then we got 'clever' by understanding the process at the papers. We still booked some full paid advertising space but also gambled on bookings being cancelled, so we went on standby at 50% of the standard rate. This enabled us to look as if we were spending more money than we were.

Another major coup in advertising the IMD Education business was using street posters. One obvious target audience for the colleges was the students completing their final high school studies and possibly not being happy with their results.

We plastered every light pole (around 5000) per city where we had a college with massive A1 size posters on the day that final school year results were released. These posters were incredibly simple with large print saying things like 'Not happy with your results, call 1800.... For career advice'. This campaign cost a relatively small amount and yielded hundreds of students on a national basis. It's interesting that the competitors did not attack us in this space for many years. It proved that being nimble and flexible allowed us to remain relevant and control our uncontested space. The thinking around most of the media campaigns that we ran, both in the South African education space and the Australian mortgage space was most certainly out-of-the-box. We were continuously searching for new, innovative and cost-effective marketing spaces.

We applied the same ideas in the mortgage business by looking for uncontested advertising space. At the time (2003/4) one of the main advertising avenues for real estate in Western Australia was a 'free' magazine called *The Home Buyer*. This was distributed at the offices of all real estate agents, generally in a stand outside their office door.

Once again, we noticed that the front page did not carry any advertising on a regular basis and that by running an advert on that page we would be front and centre for anyone walking past the real estate office. After some negotiation, they allowed us to run strip adverts on the bottom of the cover page. We virtually owned this media space for around 12 months. During that time, we were generating around 20 to25 leads per advert per week. This was very expensive given the $2500 per week price tag. However, it offered the best return on our advertising dollar at that time. It allowed the business to get and gain credibility and generate significant business due to the 70000+ distribution.

The lesson here was that the advertising space was very specific to people looking at property. Unlike the generic IMD advertising on the mainstream TV guide this was very targeted.

When Warren approached me regarding the 'Rate Detective Finance' it was unique at that time as it was a business using internet search as its focus and source of lead generation. When it started in 2009 there were a limited number of players in that space and therefore the cost of buying keywords for searches was relatively low. Over the next few years the cost per click more than doubled – it went up tenfold – making what was a relatively cheap medium very expensive. By 2012, the momentum had been generated off the internet space and that business became more mainstream in its use of traditional referral sources as opposed to internet advertising.

USE TECHNOLOGY AS A MARKETING TOOL TO INCREASE PROFESSIONALISM

One of the advantages of youth is that you tend not to over-analyse. With age, we began to look at every business decision and turn it around a million ways. It's very much a part of the google generation. We have too much information and therefore over-analyse. We keep searching for ways to make miniscule improvements so that we keep being different. Richard Branson's, *Screw it, Let's Do It* resonated with my style of management.

I had fallen into the business without much analysis or design. But once I decided to make a go of it, I was determined to be as professional as I could be. Despite wanting to appear professional, I did choose not to wear a tie. I don't believe that wearing a tie enhances my credibility, or for that matter, my professionalism. So, I still dress smart casual (chinos and a smart shirt or company polo shirt), but wear jeans on Friday. It has become such a discussion that when I wear a tie to a corporate function, there are always 'chirps' regarding my attire.

When I started the broking business in 2001, I was working from home and decided to use as much technology as I could to enhance the service offering. In line with the 'professional' philosophy that we created at IMD, I wanted to create that professional aura around me in the broking space.

I set up the following simple things to professionalise my business. I applied for a dual (called duet) line from the telephone company. This was a cheap way to have a phone number and fax number running on one line. I then permanently diverted the phone number to my mobile.

So, I was always available if anyone called the 'office line'. If I was not able to answer I diverted those calls to an answering service (answered by a real person) saying 'Rael Bricker's office. Rael is not available, please leave a message'. That message was then sent to me via SMS. So, while in a meeting, I would see the message come through and be able to respond if necessary.

The beauty of that system was that wherever I was, even when I was overseas, I received the sms. Now that I have a team, I still use the sms system when I'm overseas or in a training seminar. I can see the messages immediately and forward them to one of the team to return the call on my behalf.

Before leaving South Africa, I set up a generic email address and found something called a global dialer which allowed for dial up internet access in 100 countries. This allowed me to be connected from the first day in the new country. On one of my first visits to Australia to explore job and other opportunities, I appeared to be well advanced on the technology curve, having bought a portable printer and scanner. This later became a significant part of my 'mobile arsenal'.

In July 1999 when the family emigrated to Australia, we arrived with around 100 kg of unaccompanied luggage, including the fax machine. The beauty of technology is that once I bought a cellphone and combined that with having internet access, it allowed me to be well ahead of the technology curve.

My first blackberry in the mid 2000s also changed the game significantly – suddenly I was able to do what is common today – get email and email access on the road. It still amazes me that there are brokers who haven't yet embraced the simplest of technologies to enhance their business.

Our first port of call in the current era is *Google*. As a generalisation the world turns to google for advice on a regular basis. However, the search generally leads to many diverse opinions on a subject and we tend to use this as a basis for decision making. I find that the use of gut feel has been replaced. I try not to over-analyse decisions and trust my gut instinct.

Trusting gut instinct has consequences for your bottom line – time and money. Spending days analysing which coffee machine is the best purchase for the office should be a ten-minute decision. In reality, whatever machine you choose will be okay. A $2000 machine may last a little less time than a more expensive one, but that to spend $2000-3000 every few years on a new machine has little or no impact on the business bottom line. No coffee at all is what will really affect office productivity.

PRODUCT, PRICE, PROMOTION, PLACE

When I got to business school, one of the courses was marketing. As an engineer, that was a relatively foreign concept. The fundamental principle of marketing was based on putting the right product in the right place, at the right price, at the right time or simply product, price, promotion and place. This was called the 4P approach (was first expressed in 1960 by E J McCarthy).

Now, 30 years after first learning about that, I believe I can finally understand it. This chapter is about understanding how, on a practical level, there are many approaches to marketing and sales and how these have fundamentally shaped my approaches to business.

When we begin to analyse business and business success it becomes increasingly evident that everything is ultimately dependent on sales. To achieve sales, you need to market. Sounds simple – sales bring revenue which hopefully is in excess of costs and thereby provides profit. Sales are obviously dependent on a vast number of factors, such as the nature and quality of the product, the demand for the product, etc. However, on a simplistic level, every businessman, whether they see themselves in that way or not, is a salesman.

LEARN TO ACCEPT AND ENJOY BEING A SALESMAN

Today, I meet colleagues and competitors who see themselves as professionals in our field of finance. When I talk to them about sales skills and technique, I often get a blank stare and a response that 'I'm not a salesman'. It took me a long time to admit that I was ultimately in sales. However, the client experience needs to be a great one and potentially that can only be achieved if all the elements come together. An organisation that is focused on sales at all costs may struggle to create a positive customer experience. Like most aspects of business, there is a trade-off between getting the sale and maximising the customer experience.

In the small business context, we may prefer to be called 'marketers' rather than sales people, and that's ok. What it serves to acknowledge is that the roles in a small business are multi-functional. It's actually a key role model for larger business where marketing can't be done in isolation and needs the fundamental buy-in of all staff. I will to some extent use the terms sales and marketing interchangeably in the small business context as they are inexplicably linked even though they work fundamentally on various levels.

One of the most sophisticated salesman is the male bird. In various guises, some less flamboyant than the peacock, the male bird is, through genetics, charged with selling themselves to the females of the species. We humans are no different. We are taught to sell ourselves from an early age – parents telling children to 'make a good impression', to the later years of attraction between potential partners. It's all about selling, and selling is about finding the right product and the right price where there is a demand for that product. Some are better at sales than others.

I need to put my first longer term paying job that I got when I was 15 into some context: Around 1977 when the Citizen Band (CB radio) craze hit South Africa, I begged my parents for a CB radio. Technically CB was illegal but somehow, even in the heavily policed state of South Africa it seemed to almost be legal, or at least the police ignored the proliferation of the devices. A few of my friends had CB radios. We were probably on the younger end of the spectrum of CB users, and we all had 'cool' (or so we thought) call signs. Mine was 'radio rat'. We would all head to the C & P (choke and puke) otherwise known as the Dolls' House Roadhouse in Johannesburg for an 'eyeball' or meeting.

My father, tried to convince me not to go down that path and suggested that if I wanted to play with radios and radio communications I should go down the road of being a licensed radio ham and get my amateur radio licence. I had no real idea what that was about, but a couple who lived a few houses away had a big antenna in their garden. I walked across the road, boldly knocked on the door and asked them to tell me about Ham radio. I sat there in awe of the radio conversation about innocuous things like the weather to complete random strangers all around the world. Being able to easily eavesdrop on other people's conversations had strange appeal.

In those days, to get an amateur radio licence, the course that you had to undertake was around 10 months of one lecture per week. So, at the age of 14, I started attending these classes. I met Jon Feldman there who ultimately became my partner in two very successful business ventures. Jon and I were three months apart in age, and spent almost the entire 10 months chatting to each other through every lecture. At the end of the year, the lecturer suggested that it was unlikely that either of us would pass the exam.

We both passed the exams and got our restricted amateur radio licences. My call sign was zr6xw. To get to the next stage of 'unrestricted licence', I had to pass a test in morse code proficiency at 12 words per minute.

It was at this stage that I got my first real job. I started working at an electronics shop in downtown Johannesburg called Hamrad Electronics on most Saturdays and school holidays. The shop was divided into two areas – selling electronic components and selling ham radio equipment. It was here that I began my sales journey.

In the shop, the sales process was predominantly reactive. Customers would walk into the shop and ask for a particular component. We would then find the product or suggest a suitable alternative. A small minority of customers would walk in and ask for advice. The advice ranged from specific questions on an aspect of a project to areas around repair of electronic devices. We were often asked about a particular project or advice on an installation (such as a car radio/music). The latter was possibly one of the few times when selling and upselling came into the picture as the clients were generally undecided about what they were looking for. Even at that stage, we understood the cross-sell and up-sell of offering better products or associated products to the clients.

McDonalds is a good example of the art of the cross-sell with the 'do you want fries with that?' It's such an innocuous question, and most people love fries, so the add-on is a relatively easy sell. The $1 upgrade to your soft drink is also an effective up-sell.

Everyone in this world is a salesman, or more politically correct, sales person. I'm not referring to the job of being in sales, but rather the ability to influence others to a particular course of action.

It took me many years in several businesses to acknowledge that I had the ability to sell. When I was at Hamrad there were no individual measures of sales performance. The group of sales people were lumped together. It was easy to hide and be unproductive.

How did I learn to accept and enjoy being a salesman? I discovered that I could never be a 'hard sell salesman' and that all my selling is backed by an intrinsic belief in the product and service, coupled with a soft sell approach.

What is easier to sell – products or services?

And, does it matter?

There is a concept in marketing called 'selling the sizzle'. Successful restaurants are selling everything around the product that enhances the product. Coke are famous for selling the 'feeling'. In my two most successful businesses we sold services in very different ways, but closely connected.

If I think back to my time in the education business, and now the mortgage business, it was about selling services. There may have been a tangible outcome (a qualification or home ownership), but this is neither here nor there when it is related to the actual sales process.

BELIEVE IN YOUR PRODUCT OR SERVICE

Many of my 'referrers' would ask me to 'get the clients over the line'. My style is to sell without seeming to sell. That means I have to be convinced about the service I offer.

Part of the process of working with my clients is to be neutral. I am agnostic. It raises some eyebrows until I explain that I am agnostic regarding which property they buy and would use the same strategies and structures irrespective of the actual property. This helps the clients to decide. The decision is around the choice to buy an investment property without feeling the pressure from the sales person. In most cases, the fundamental decision to buy a property was harder to make than the decision of which property to buy. My role is to facilitate the decision to buy in the first place by looking at the general structures and strategies around that decision. Once the clients had made the decision to move ahead, based on their unique specific circumstances, they were then referred back to the source (referrer) to decide on what to buy.

The question is what techniques do we use to help the client make the choice to buy a property? After all, if the client chooses not to buy, then we don't get paid. However, I have always believed, and trained my team to believe, that the ultimate decision must be made by the client. We can only facilitate the facts and figures to a level, and then the client must make a final decision. In fact, our success is largely positioned on this soft sell approach. A large part of the process is establishing our credibility to discuss all the options with the client.

This positioning as an expert establishes credibility to get clients to listen and follow. This is encapsulated in a variety of ways such as:

I am outspoken on the fundamental value of our service, and on a broader level the service that the mortgage brokers as a general group supply to the public. In the first brochure for House & Home Loans, written by Jon and I in 2004, we made the comment that if the service given by a broker does not add to the costs, 'why would you not use a broker'. The mortgage industry has shifted to a situation where in 2017 more than 55% of mortgages in Australia are written by brokers. This reinforces the principles we established many years ago.

In the education business, we were selling the idea that we were the best at ensuring the students were delivered a qualification. The service we were delivering was one of enabling the students to achieve a tangible outcome and obtain a qualification. At the IMD Education Centres, we, as the owners, and the staff were so convinced by our ability to deliver. This was encapsulated in our enthusiasm for what we did. This genuine enthusiasm was the spark that I believe ignited the passion with which we sold ourselves and our services.

I believe we established this belief in ourselves as a core fundamental principal in the mortgage business. Over the years we have received many industry accolades and awards that validate to some extent, our belief in being one of the best. Once again, we deliver a service that is somewhat intangible and is evidenced by a mortgage on a bank statement, but is used to facilitate the acquisition of a tangible asset being a property.

I like to give clients some personal information about myself. It breaks barriers and allows them to feel comfortable talking to me. As an aside, this often puts clients at ease enough to disclose information about themselves that they were not planning on divulging. Obviously when representing a client in making an application for finance it is core to our integrity to disclose all that we know. Therefore, enabling the clients to feel at ease is one way of ensuring the best result for all concerned.

~~~~~

HARD SELL

A classic example of hard selling occurred on the last day of the financial year of 2015. I was contemplating changing my gym to the gym near the office. I had a few minutes and popped in to get an idea of pricing options. The last time I signed up at my current gym they had a written list of pricing and options that they gave me to take away.

I was asked to wait for one of the membership consultants who arrived with a tablet device. He asked some details, and then hit a few buttons and showed me a summary of a rate per week to join the gym.

I asked him to email the details to me – he replied that they could not do that, and that as a 'special' if I signed up that day he would reduce the rate by $3.50 per week. I indicated that I was not ready to sign up as I wanted to find out how long was still left on my current gym contract.

By the end of that day I had received 3 SMS messages offering me a 'free period' of a few months to overlap with the exiting contract if I signed up on that day.

KEEP IT SIMPLE

Another aspect of client communication revolves around developing a method of explaining fairly complex finance to clients in easy-to-understand pictures. The team use the pictures and some numbers to explain the fundamentals and check back on their understanding of these basic concepts. The use of simple colour-coded pictures engages with the clients in simple terms and allows them to (hopefully) understand complex structures in simple ways.

The soft sell process is refined and elegant. When I meet with a client the meeting is about me taking old fashioned pen and paper notes. This process of keeping it simple is a very powerful part of our sales arsenal. Sometimes I use an iPad, but use a note-taking app. This allows me to talk freely to the clients, ask questions that would be specific to their circumstances, and generally gain credibility through subtle displays of knowledge and wisdom. I either draw the pictures on paper using coloured pens or on a notepad app on the iPad.

One of the biggest referrers to my mortgage business has refined the soft sell approach, in a market dominated by hard sell spruikers. I have worked with many real estate agents over time. Many of whom are the stereotypical 'pushy real estate salesman'. They find the faintest glimmer of interest and nurture that to get the sale.

This referral group, however, invites potential clients to free public seminars on property and investing. Over the years I have spoken at hundreds of these workshops. No direct selling was done at these introductory workshops. The format of the workshop was and still is around a series of presentations on various topics such as 'what does your retirement look like on a pension?', 'why invest in real estate?', 'what to look for in real estate investment?'. These were interspersed with one or two personal journeys of people who had followed the principles and built up a portfolio of properties.

At these workshops, I would present anywhere from a ten-minute informal presentation to a one-hour formal presentation. The formal presentations covered topics such as the actual process of building a portfolio or funding your retirement portfolio amongst others. The sole objective of these introductory workshops was to generate interest and credibility. The latter was through our display of knowledge and confidence around the finance.

Most of these workshops at the introductory level are run in the evenings. One of my favourite openings to a presentation for this referrer, is to start with the question 'how is it that I can be excited about finance at this time of night?' I then answer the question with the statement that 'I am excited because each one of you has a specific and unique set of circumstances and poses unique challenges to me as a broker'.

At the workshops, clients are encouraged, within the privacy laws, to provide a summary of their personal financial circumstances. We (as the brokers) can quickly analyse their situation and give them an approximate idea of how much they could borrow. This then opens the door for a conversation between the sales team, from the referral group, and the clients about finding a suitable investment within their budget. Additionally, it is about opening the door for us, as the brokers, to have a conversation with a potential client. We as the brokers worked closely with the sales team to 'get the clients over the line'. A big part of the sales process is the long-term nature of the relationship where clients are not clients but 'club members'. This is probably why we have worked together for so long (14 years) as we both use very soft sell techniques in dealing with potential clients.

One of my most valuable sales techniques over the years that formed a cornerstone of the soft sell approach was around specific deliverable outcomes for a client. In 99% of discussions with clients, I end the meeting with a promise to do some work on their numbers and respond back to them by a specific time. The reality is that in most cases, I would know exactly what the right structure would look like and which lender would be appropriate. However, by taking 24 hours, I found I could cross check myself and soften the approach. In addition, to being less pushy, whether I actually did more work on the numbers or not, it was most certainly a way of establishing further credibility with the clients. One of the tips is the idea that communication is king. This starts in my business when the client is a prospect and not yet a client. If I commit to replying to them by a date or time, I can say that in 99% of cases I have managed to meet these self-imposed deadlines. There is always the 1% where we miss the self-imposed deadlines, and that is the area that we focus on for self-improvement.

COMMUNICATION IS KING

The approach of pen and paper and 'working on their numbers' is in direct contrast to one of the largest mortgage franchise operations in Australia. Their advertising campaign was centred on the notion of 'our consultants will come to you, input your data into our software and the software will tell you the best deal'. What always struck me was that we needed to be different. This approach told you nothing about the quality of the consultant, and in fact relegated the consultant to data capturer. By contrast, our training approach with brokers was, and still is, the use of pen and paper notes (or iPad note-taking software.) The key difference is that we ask and discuss with clients their needs and objectives without the computer being a tool between us. This serves to create a high level of trust as clients get to know our knowledge base and our value-add, rather than the software. The brokers from our team establish themselves as the knowledgeable experts rather than showing reliance on the software packages. We relegate the software to the background and showcase the knowledge and experience of the brokers.

This is very different to the two almost distinct approaches to real estate sales that I have encountered over the years. The first approach is the 'transactional approach'. This is where you go and view a property and provide the real estate agent with some basic parameters (bedrooms bathrooms, etc). If you indicate that the property is not for you, the questions revolve around 'what is wrong with this property?

By contrast, the realtor who is 'people focused', will ask questions around 'what are you looking for?' In the end, you as a potential buyer may provide the same information, but now it is focused not only on the negatives of the property, but on the positives.

The real estate business in Australia has changed significantly over the years. When we arrived in 1999, and started looking for a house, my wife and I met several real estate agents. One way of finding a property was to find the agent that you liked, and they would look at all available properties in your market and take a personally conducted tour of these properties. This was irrespective of the agent who had listed the property for sale. They would then share in the commission with the listing agent. This was a form of buyer's agent, although ultimately the payment was made by the vendor, not the buyer. Sadly, this tacit agreement between realtors no longer works.

A large car dealership in Perth that handles many brands of car, recently started an advertising campaign based around this idea. They advertise 'choose your dealer before you choose your car'. This group has a family patriarch who is a Perth icon and been in the motor business for many years. The entire campaign, spoken by the family patriarch is about using 'WA's most trusted dealer'. The reality is that most customers won't deal with the patriarch, but his pitch as the most trusted dealer puts his team on an elevated pedestal.

I have bought and sold several cars. The sales process in the motor dealerships has been a learning experience and, at times, probably an expensive one. A general observation is that when the economy was booming in Western Australia (pre-GFC 2008) the human factor in most sales organisations, such as vehicles and real estate, was non-existent. Real estate agents collected data at home opens, but due to demand for houses and the quick turnaround in sales, never really followed up with potential buyers. The car yards, followed much the same pattern. I noticed that post-GFC, the number of return calls from car salesmen was much higher as they needed to chase business that was no longer walking through the door.

For me, selling the intangible, or services, is this area that I am most comfortable with and have found that a soft sell approach to be effective for me.

LEARN TO SAY 'I DON'T KNOW'

'When someone asks you a question that you don't know the answer to, mumble, excuse yourself and run to find an expert who does know the answer'. I knew nothing about electronics and electronic components when I started at Hamrad, but I learned quickly by osmosis. I was quite happy to serve at the sales counter and when someone asked for something that I had no idea about, I would go to the back, find a colleague who knew and revert with the correct information. When training my staff today, I always encourage them not to be afraid of saying 'I don't know' or 'I'm not sure', followed by 'I will find out'.

≈≈≈

An expert is not always the one who knows the answer, but knows where to find the answer.

If you have already established credibility with clients, they won't be bothered by you not knowing one particular fact. Having all the information at your fingertips is not important, but the ability and willingness to get the information quickly and interpret it correctly is essential.

In my mortgage business, I am often asked for information that is well outside of the scope of anything I can and am licensed to give advice on. As an example, clients looking at selling a property will ask specific questions about their capital gains tax in relation to the current transaction.

My first answer, and I hope the one all my staff give is 'it's best to consult with your tax accountant as he (or she) has the specific details of your tax situation.' I may then go on to explain the basic principles of capital gains using a generic example rather than their specific one. This serves multiple purposes:

- It maintains my credibility with the client as it establishes my understanding of the information

- It acknowledges the role of a fellow professional in dealing with a mutual client

- It allows me to say that 'I don't know the answer in detail', but in a subtle way

- From a legal perspective, I am on record as not giving advice outside of the scope that I am allowed

In July 2015, an article appeared in the mortgage industry press based on a lobby organisation criticising brokers for being salesmen. *The Adviser* magazine countered with an article saying brokers should position themselves as educators not salesmen. At the end of the day, I think that we are all ultimately salesmen. But the most compliments I get from clients are around the fact that I explain finance in layman's terms that they can understand.

I would guess then, I use the education of the clients to convince them to see why my solution is the best (and I get the sale from that).

CHAPTER 6
FIND SOURCES OF KNOWLEDGE AND MENTORING

~~~~

One of the tag lines of the 'MasterChef' TV show (Australia) is 'extraordinary cooking from ordinary cooks'. That is my view on many of the people I have met and who have influenced me. There were some incredible high achievers revered by society, who helped and assisted me in numerous ways. However, the day to day interactions with 'ordinary' people are as important as the high achievers.

I have always been fiercely independent. I have never been able to follow a particular mentor to the exclusion of all others. However, over many years in business I have had countless influencers and influences:

This chapter will look at aspects of:

- Always learning from those around you
- Finding people who can give you knowledge or skills at a particular time
- Paying it forward and paying it back

DO THINGS FOR NO REWARD – JUST BECAUSE YOU CAN

One of the guys who worked at Hamrad was Reg Green. Reg was one of the original radio hams in the South Africa. He was a radio operator in the war and used to have conversations in morse code every Saturday morning at the shop. He could be having a 'conversation' with his friend overseas and could talk to customers in the shop, while simultaneously sending and receiving morse code. To Reg, listening and sending morse code was no different to listening to two conversations at once. The lesson I learnt was that the brain has the innate ability to multitask.

Reg was probably also one of my earliest influences in sales and sales techniques. In the field of Ham radio there were not many more knowledgeable people than Reg, however in every customer interaction (and colleague interaction) he was able to impart knowledge in a way that was educational and presented on a peer level basis. Many people who have superior knowledge of a product or service often lack the ability to impart that knowledge to others without a seemingly superior attitude. The sales person in a store should have superior knowledge of a particular product or service if they are to be successful. The most successful sales people will communicate that knowledge in a way that educates the potential buyer in a way that does not make them feel inferior. Reg was very good at this and was able to communicate the various aspects of the equipment we were selling in a way that never made him look superior to the potential customer.

Explaining concepts in their terms and language makes clients feel empowered – a technique I learned from Reg at the tender age of 15 .

I had to learn morse code to get my unrestricted radio license, and Reg suggested a teacher that would assist me (over the radio) in the evening to practice. Felix was blind. He worked as a telephone operator at Anglo American Corporation (where I would work years later). I never met him in person, but spent many hours talking to him over the radio in plain English and morse code. He was patient and prepared to spend time with a 16-year-old boy, teaching an obscure skill set for no reward other than the pleasure of passing on the skill. This was a valuable lesson in altruism and giving back. Despite his disability, he was always chirpy and positive and viewed every day as a new challenge, thankful for being alive and being able to work and help others. I never really worked out how he operated his radio transceivers, and for that matter the switchboard at a major corporation.

SPEAK OUT

In my teenage years, I discovered an ability to speak in public. Throughout school I was always outspoken and never afraid to have my say. This probably got me into trouble over the years for having a 'big mouth'.

My father, who passed away in 1999 after many years of illness was always a very good public speaker. He started taking me with him to Toastmasters meetings at around the age of 15. In the Toastmasters club there were a wide range of people in a wide range of jobs whose creative outlet was public speaking. At this forum, we learned from our own speeches and those of others, by listening to the speeches and then the evaluations. It was probably at Toastmasters that I established my confidence on stage and my ability to speak in public. It always strikes me as strange when people say that they fear public speaking.

One of the strongest speaking skills developed at Toastmasters was the area of impromptu speaking. We were given a topic unseen and asked to speak for approximately three minutes on the spot on that topic. One of the most successful techniques I learned from those speakers was how they could recall a humorous story or joke, modify it to meet the topic and expand it to fill the time. I decided that I would try and develop that skill. Over the years I have developed this ability to store away and recall a joke, punchline or quote at a moment's notice. I must thank all my speaking mentors over the years who helped me develop and hone these skills.

NETWORK WITH RESPECT

On one of my early visits to Perth prior to emigrating I met David Schwartz, through his sister Lynn whom I knew from Johannesburg. I was in Perth over a weekend and was invited by David for Friday evening Sabbath (Shabbat) dinner. At the time I was contemplating coming to Perth and starting a branch of an international education franchise called Academy of Learning. I have a very clear recollection of a hot February night in Perth and after dinner standing outside in the breeze chatting. At that time David advised me to come to Perth and 'find a job'. He said that the best thing I could do was get a job for 6-12 months after arriving to understand the Australian way of doing things and find my feet. As it so happened, David was intimately involved in helping me find my first job in Australia a few months later.

A few weeks after arriving in Perth, I contacted David and asked him if he could review my resume and point me in the direction of some employment. I went to meet him at his factory on a Friday morning in late July 1999 and we discussed my experience and skill set. He said he would give it some thought. On Sunday around lunchtime, we were having a family picnic at Trigg Beach and David called me to say that he had a friend who ran a venture capital firm that would like to meet me, and would I be available at around 4pm for him to fetch me and take me to meet his friend?

David fetched me and took me to meet John Schaffer at his house in Claremont. Only afterwards did I realise that David and John were shareholders and directors of Loftus Pooled Development. At the end of that evening I was offered a job as 'investment manager' of this young fund. A few days later I started at the fund and met the third of the three key directors, John Abernethy. All three proved to be fantastic mentors and made my landing in Australia very easy and gave me a foot up in business. To this day, I can still call on them for advice and assistance when necessary.

I have always been a networker and not been shy to call on people I have met for assistance in a variety of ways. What I discovered from the Loftus team was their extensive network of contacts and how to treat those contacts with respect. Since 1999 in Perth I have honed my networking skills and hope that I have created a very strong network of my own, both locally and nationally.

In terms of networking, my staff are amused at how I manage to go through 2000+ business cards per year. Mostly it is about networking, but a major portion is about promotion of the business and hopefully generating new clients. Australia is profoundly influenced by its major trading partners in Asia, and I have always been intrigued by the Asian protocol of handing a business card to people showing your credentials. I do this often, and hopefully in the correct way.

As an added marketing bonus, I often hand out two cards with the line 'my marketing guys said I must give you one for a friend'. Many marketing and sales experts tell you to ask for referrals. I find this quite a subtle way of asking for referrals, without specifically asking and quite aligned with my soft sell approach.

PAY IT FORWARD

Today, through the network in Perth, I often assist new immigrants with contacts and opportunities to help make their landing in Perth as smooth as mine was. I do this for no other reason than to pay it forward. To take what I learned from David and John assisting me, as I believe that by assisting others now, they will help others in the future and pay it forward. I mentioned to a friend who had arrived in Perth a few months after we did that I was writing this book and moving into the public speaking arena. He asked me for some information on what areas I was speaking on so that he could give it to his group chief executive. He said that in early 2000 I had helped him find his first job in Perth and this was his way of paying back.

Chapter 7

Tolerance and Understanding

≋

—

No one is born hating another person because of the colour of his skin, or his background, or his religion. People must learn to hate, and if they can learn to hate, they can be taught to love, for love comes more naturally to the human heart than its opposite.

— Nelson Mandela

—

Like most lessons in our early life, I only appreciated the lessons learnt working on the mines much later. Of fundamental importance was being tolerant of other people, how everyone is different and how you deal with that. There are many different stories that illustrate this idea.

One of my main drivers in life is pride in being Jewish. In terms of religious observance, I would call myself and my family traditional orthodox Jews. I don't eat pork, shellfish or venison and I observe almost all festivals. In other words, although I don't follow a strictly kosher diet, whenever I'm invited out, I advise my hosts of my dietary requirements. On the mines, there was a tradition of having a loss control party at each safety milestone. Every time the mine (or on a smaller level a site or workspace) hit a milestone of a certain number of days 'injury free' (or on a more morbid level – death free) days they would throw a party. At this event there would be free-flowing alcohol and most of the staff would drink to excess and then drive home. An ironic and weird concept related to loss of control!

In terms of food they would always have a braai or barbecue. At the time, most of my colleagues would jokingly say that they were putting on a special for me of 'vark tjops' and 'spek wors' (literally pig chops and pork sausages). At the time, as a 21-year-old junior employee I embraced that as somewhat of a joke. In retrospect, I believe some would have seen it as disrespectful at best, anti-semitic at worst.

Being proud of my Jewish heritage has shaped many of my life philosophies and views of the world. Growing up in South Africa, particularly Johannesburg where the Jewish population was strong and of significant size, it was easy to be Jewish. There was very little anti-Semitic sentiment and the pre-1990 South Africa almost allowed people to be racists. This allowed most people who would in today's world be anti-Jewish or anti-Israel to channel their 'anger' towards the majority black population rather than the Jews. I'm by no means justifying the apartheid government of the time, but suggesting that as a minority (Jewish) of a minority (white South Africans) we were somewhat protected and shielded.

When I got to the mines, I was the only Jewish employee of 50 000 staff (or the only one vocal enough to stand up for being Jewish). What I realised is that a lot of people there, who had grown up in the country (where there was a small Jewish population) had not really had any business contact with Jews, let alone any social contact.

There were two reactions to my overt Jewishness. The one was a genuine interest, driven by Christian beliefs and a desire to understand something of the differences and similarities between Judaism and Christianity. South Africa of the apartheid years was always driven by a strong church influence in government and society. The second group were those who believed in the traditional laager mentality, ie anyone who is different is bad.

The laager mentality grew out of South African history from the times of the Great Trek. During that time, groups of disgruntled Afrikaners travelled via oxwagon from the coastal sections of South Africa to the interior or hinterland. They would move during the day and form the wagons into a circle for protection called a laager at night. In the USA during similar expansionary times in history when wagon trains 'went out west' the pioneers also formed circles for protection. The term 'circling the wagons' is used as an English description of the 'Laager'. However, this mentality of 'those who are outside the circle (laager) are the enemy' morphed into a philosophy of 'all who are outside are the enemy', a not so subtle change of the addition of the word all. This mentality has been part of one of the cultural shaping factors of South Africa both pre-and post-democratic government. Possibly this same idea of intolerance towards anyone who is different is or 'outside' could be linked to most world conflicts historically and is still prevalent today.

NEVER ASK STAFF TO DO ANYTHING I WOULD NOT DO

The other key lesson from this time on the mines was learning all aspects of a job. In the mining environment, the engineer, whether on the plant or shaft is ultimately responsible for all trades, both mechanical and electrical. This comprised the electricians (something I had some knowledge of as I was studying electrical engineering) and fitters and boilermakers (mechanical). It was quite a shock to me that an electrical engineer (or mechanical for that matter) would ultimately oversee all engineering aspects, albeit not their area of specialty.

You had to learn to do all aspects of the job, sometimes even beyond the parameters of the job itself. This levels the playing fields and creates an atmosphere of equality and fairness in the workplace. It's far easier to be tolerant when you know exactly what a colleague is experiencing.

Often, I'm in the office after hours and my admin team have quit for the night. When I or another team member has a meeting with a client, I make a point of making tea and coffee myself (for the client). If the same appointment was during the day, one of my admin team would make the drinks. I probably don't make as good a cappuccino as my staff, but they see me doing the most basic of tasks and appreciate the effort. It also makes them willing to do it when asked.

When we started the IMD education centres, Jon and I did everything – from typing the notes for students, standing at the copier making the copies, punching and binding them for handouts to the students and, of course, being the lecturers as well. Not for one second in the early days did we see any of these tasks as below us. Rather, the way they were performed was to set the standards as we began to employ staff and delegated some of these aspects of the business.

The same logic applies in all business – we are never expected to be masters of all aspects of our business, but must have and maintain enough understanding of each and every task in the organisation.

After about 19 months of working on Vaal Reefs, I managed to arrange a transfer to head office in Johannesburg. When I got to the head office, the only office available on our floor was a corner office with views. At that stage I had no understanding of corporate politics or protocols and happily moved into the office as it was allocated to me. It took me a while to become part of the team as I first had to deal with the politics of why the new guy, a junior, 'got the corner office'. It was ironic because I never aspired to the 'corner office' and never really saw myself as a long-term employee of a huge corporation.

The most concrete lessons from my time at Anglo (both mines and head office) was never to give the junior the corner office!

But I also knew I never wanted to be part of a large corporation, I knew I wanted to be the boss, or master, of my own destiny. In a number of instances this driving force has been my downfall and stopped me seeing all opportunities.

HAVE A FUN WORK ENVIRONMENT

I always wanted to create an organisation where people like to work, have fun and have a laugh. I think the ability to laugh and joke (whilst being politically sensitive – if not correct all the time) is a critical aspect of business success. Laughter has many documented benefits, and there are even therapists who use laughter therapy. One of my colleagues from another broking firm calls me the Segue king, as I always manage to find an aspect of a conversation as a hook to segue into a joke or humorous story. Good-natured humour can often be the bridge between differing workstyles and personalities.

CHAPTER 8

DIVERSITY AND DIVERSITY INTELLIGENCE

If we cannot end now our differences, at least we can help make the world safe for diversity. For in the final analysis our most basic common link is that we all inhabit this planet. We all breathe the same air. We all cherish our children's future. We are all mortal.

JOHN F KENNEDY

Our ability to reach unity in diversity will be the beauty and test of our civilisation

MAHATMA GANDHI

Once the ideas of embracing tolerance and having an understanding of all the people around you has been established, then making the leap to diversity intelligence becomes a small hop.

WHAT IS DIVERSITY?

It sounds simple to define diversity. But the reality is Shrek's analogy of an onion with its multitude of layers. An organisation trying to define diversity will be confused by the fine layers. I recently met an expert in current diversity thinking who pointed out some of the obvious issues. She indicated that she was female and therefore a corporate minority group. However, as a black woman, she formed a subset of the diversity tree. So, from an organised diversity system, it becomes tricky on how to define her group.

This intersectionality of various sub-groups poses a challenge to organisations that espouse a policy of embracing and encouraging diversity. In Australia, over the last few years, the diversity movement has been based around three broad categories, namely, race, gender and age. It's a suitable place to start, however it fails to recognise some of the subtle characteristics of diversity. Diversity programmes are about recognising the differences between people and embracing these differences.

WHAT IS DIVERSITY INTELLIGENCE?

DI (Diversity Intelligence) is loosely defined as the ability to synergise the diversity of culture across an organisation to make the organisation stronger and more efficient. In the military, for reasons of command and control, people from diverse backgrounds are pushed through a 'sausage machine' in order to make them all the same. The rationale is that in a military situation, it is critically important that all the soldiers respond to a given command in the same manner. In the corporation, we would hope that the leadership are issuing 'commands' in such a way that it embraces the strengths and diversity of the team.

Diversity intelligence harnesses these differences rather than trying to normalise them. The idea of diversity and inclusion looks to make organisations stronger in terms of relations internally within the teams and externally with other stakeholders.

SHOULD RACE, GENDER AND AGE BE THE CRITERIA?

Just as each person in a room presents a separate set of financial circumstances, each one would also be represented by a different spot on any measures of diversity. It is those unique set of circumstances that can provide interest and challenge.

One of the most iconic symbols of Australia, and particularly the red centre is Uluru, known in English as Ayers Rock. Interestingly, Uluru is 348m tall, and it is considered that it stretches more than 2.5km or more into the ground. If we divide this into three areas and look at the diversity analogy along these lines, the section stretching above the ground is the obvious iconic part and visible. The section close to the ground is somewhat visible, but not always, whereas the bulk of Uluru is hidden under the ground. These three aspects illustrate that 90% of 'who we are' is hidden below the surface.

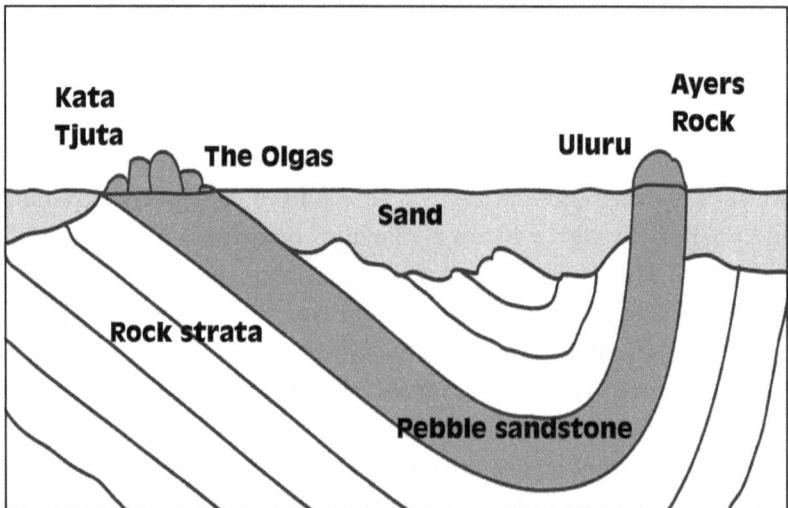

Over the years, psychologists and others have used similar versions of this model, using an iceberg as the analogy. The main difference is that icebergs tend to move and often collide below the surface where 90% of their bulk is hidden. So too do people clash on their below-the-surface characteristics because doing so above the line is seen as prejudice or overt bias, either on gender or race.

Above the ground we see the obvious and not so obvious differences. These are broadly classified as gender, race and age. This could further be broken down into categories such as dress style, appearance, etc.

Then, there are the diversity measures on the ground level. Depending on the day and other conditions, sometimes these are visible and other times hidden. Some of these would include nationality, ethnicity, religion, wealth, social status, sexual orientation and the list goes on. A simple understanding of this could be around religious symbols or statements of faith or ethnicity. Someone wearing a burka, Sikh turban or Jewish skullcap (yarmulke) would all be expressing outwardly some level of religious or cultural affiliation. By the same token there are undoubtedly many more people who share the same religious or cultural affiliation but do not display the outward signs. This is where the ground level becomes increasingly murky.

In the mortgage industry, there is increasing pressure on lenders to be responsible. For example, if a potential mortgage client being interviewed is female and appears, from physical signs, to be pregnant it poses a challenge. The challenge is to ascertain the information without asking biased questions.

The lending challenge is that in most cases when a woman gives birth, there is a period when they are not in the workforce. This time may adversely affect their ability to meet their financial commitments. The questions asked are phrased in terms of 'do you foresee any short or medium-term changes in income or employment?'

A rather embarrassing incident happened in the early 2000s when I was a rookie finance broker. I asked a client, at a first meeting, whether she was pregnant. Her attitude changed, and she left the room at which time her partner explained that the baby was 6 months old and that she had been struggling to regain her pre-baby figure. My insensitivity ensured that I did not get the business. The lesson learned was to be more tactful and show more emotional intelligence.

Below the ground the hidden characteristics and criteria differ vastly. The ideas can range from values and heritage to family status and education. Every writer around this topic lists a multitude of options for the diversity below the ground. These are no less important than the above-the-line characteristics. However, many of these are subjective and could potentially revolve around attitudes, beliefs and feelings.

A current, very topical debate in Australia has been around the 2017 plebiscite on whether the constitution should change to allow for same sex marriage. This cost $100m and was voluntary and non-binding on the government. Essentially it was a way for the government to avoid the direct issue of having a conscience vote rather than the traditional votes along party lines. In my own direct reporting team of 11, there was some animated debate from various team members and their preferences. The team is incredibly diverse, with team members from five countries and an almost even gender split. It also encompasses racial and ethnic diversity.

Regarding the plebiscite, there are many reports of intense debates in companies, where the leaders wished to support one of the viewpoints as a corporate. I think the actual benefit of the process is that it has helped to highlight diversity and in many cases, assist in getting people communicating about the above and below the surface issues.

The challenge for you is to step back and look at your organisation. How much do you know about the below the ground issues of your team?

DIVERSITY – IS IT COMPLEX?

It is time for parents to teach young people early on that in diversity there is beauty and there is strength.

MAYA ANGELOU

Given the complexity of defining the layers of diversity, how do organisations define their diversity initiatives? Should organisations attempt to define their diversity objectives on a small number of measures? In South Africa where I grew up, these diversity initiatives were first defined on race, with specific diversity targets based on black ownership and representation across the organisation. Today they still rest on black empowerment initiatives, but have an added layer of gender equality requirements.

In August 2017 I gave a talk at the Wits Business School in Johannesburg. At the completion of the talk, during question time, I was asked whether I thought that the BEE (Black Economic Empowerment) initiatives had worked and yielded success. I prefaced my answer with the fact that I had been living in Australia since 1999 and therefore thought that the question was somewhat out of my direct experience.

However, the sub-text of that question was whether BEE had worked to a point where people of colour were being promoted on merit rather than on the colour of their skin. My answer was that I could not comment with any certainty on the South African situation.

However, I believe that we are probably a generation away from an ideal utopia where diversity is no longer an issue. People can be promoted on pure merit when an organisation no longer needs quotas to ensure that there is diversity. And ironically, this is when real diversity can happen. But this is part of the problem.

The very concept of diversity requires that people are classified into sub- groups. We then expend tons of energy in trying to use the diversity to the benefit of the organisation. We work at using the cultural differences for diversity intelligence. There seems to be a contradiction here.

I believe that diversity in organisations and the synergistic energy that that brings together is vital for success. Diversity intelligence is how we embrace the diversity of the organisation to use the variety and experiences to enhance the collective. In an ideal world, we would be able to naturally have an organisation that is diverse by whatever measures we are using.

Herein lies the problem and the challenge. Human nature is such that we tend to try and surround ourselves with people who are like us.

One interesting phenomenon is in large cities, where you'll usually find a 'little Italy' or 'Chinatown'. How does this enhance diversity? Or does it merely promote people of diverse cultures eating different foods. Or does it really show that people tend to revert to a comfort zone where they are surrounded by people like themselves. Does this lead to a problem? Does it mean that our default position is to avoid diversity?

No, it does not. It means that we can still have a community. A community that acts and thinks like we do. After all, that is our comfortable place. How is that community defined?

In November 2017 I was invited to a fantastic retreat conference in Franschoek in the Western Cape (South Africa). The theme was reconciliation and diversity intelligence and its impact on making the world a better place – a place of harmony and acceptance and embracing of diversity.

The question of a place of comfort was challenged by an attending church leader. He was attempting to define, in a humorous manner, what the not so subtle difference was between two branches of the same church. This highlighted to me the deeper issue – we cannot even rely on broad religious affiliation (or any other category) to define our community or even our diversity.

But the challenge outside that comfortable place is to fit in to a place where we don't all think alike or have the same cultural or ethnic backgrounds.

When we look at the greater organisation we need to address the process and concepts around diversity. We can expand the concept of the organisation to our community, city, country and in an ideal time, the world.

If we are all equal, then should the word 'minority' even apply? How do we take out the word 'minority' from the diversity lexicon? Or for that matter, should we remove the concept of a minority?

In the November/December 2017 edition of Harvard Business Review, Maxine Williams, in talking about diversity by statistics comments 'If only there were more of you, we could tell you why there are so few of you'. Maxine Williams is the Facebook Global Director of Diversity. She continues with the idea that 'Statistics don't capture what it feels like to be the only black team member'.

There have been several articles written about how, in the USA (but assumed to be a worldwide phenomenon) there are specific job categories or departments that attract particular racial or ethnic groupings. The articles suggest that this is linked to the comments by Maxine Williams where it is easier to fit in if there are some similar people in that department or silo.

How does this play out in helping to create all-inclusive diversity intelligence? I'm afraid that it does not. The challenge for organisations is to look beyond the numbers. Employers need to break down the barriers and find ways to ensure that minority group employees don't feel like statistics that have to be filled and don't feel like the comment by Maxine Williams on 'being the only black team member'.

STARTING THE CLIMB TO DIVERSITY

There are many people who have inspired me over the years. I am also inspired by many places. Jerusalem is one of those places. I acknowledge that whilst it may not be perfect, it is a multi-cultural melting pot of religions and cultures, within the only true democracy in the middle east.

It is a place where you walk on the old stone paths up the old stone steps and past the old stone walls. A place where signs on those ancient stone walls point out special places for many religious groups. These signs, as are many around Israel, are in three languages. Hebrew, Arabic and English. It would be wonderful if the world embraced diversity like that.

B

M

I

L

C

Walking up those old stone steps, you realise the extent of history, both good and bad that has gone before you. However, I also realised that these old stone steps should tell a story. One that embraces history, whilst looking forwards and upwards. The story is one of how we can elevate ourselves and our organisations and our communities and by extension of countries and our world. Why do we want to elevate them? We want to elevate them to a higher place of diversity intelligence and embracing differences.

In that regard, I have developed a process model for us to use in starting the journey of discovery. It is for starting the CLIMB upwards to a better place of inclusion and diversity.

THE CLIMB MODEL

What follows is a summary of a more detailed process of team engagement strategies:

THE C – STARTING POINT

As leaders we need to COMMIT to the journey. This commitment needs to be real, and start the journey to a place where the team are committed to be a part of the process.

Getting the commitment of the team starts with COMMU-NICATION. The communication challenge is to encourage team members to explore both the differences and similarities between each other.

The team members are CHALLENGED to move out of their comfort zones. They are challenged to communicate with team members with whom they may not communicate normally.

COMMUNITY is another aspect of this step. It is vital for several reasons. One is that everybody needs a safe place to revert, such as their community. It also embraces the idea of forming a new community over time, based on a new set of values and beliefs around a specific area.

CONTEMPLATION is a necessary part of the process. It may be a quite detailed and complex process to embrace the diversity and, therefore, some time out is necessary. Some religions call this time out the Sabbath or Day of Rest. Steven Covey refers to 'Sharpening the Saw'. Whatever your comfort zone – this resting and recharging is a necessary step in the process.

THE L STEP

Moving from the C to the L takes us up a notch in actions. It expands on the actions started in the previous step.

The previous step suggested starting the process of communication. Here we specifically LISTEN to each other. Along with this we start to LOOK at each other through different lenses. The combination of listening and looking should help us get to a point of actually LIKING each other. In the ideal utopian world that extends to LOVE.

The LEADERS need to embrace the process and keep leading from the front whilst encouraging the team to keep up. There is concept of leading from the rear, and it comes down to a leadership style where we can push people up the steps or pull them along with us. In embracing diversity, it may make more sense to pull them up and as leaders we are leading by example.

THE MIDDLE STEP OR I

This is the middle of the journey, where possibly the end is not yet in sight. The leader needs to continue to INSPIRE the team. When it is hard to see the end of the journey the team needs inspiration to enjoy the journey without so much focus on the destination.

This may require some INNOVATION from the leaders to keep the team moving to a place in the future.

The team needs to start to INCULCATE a culture of embracing the diversity amongst us.

ALMOST AT THE TOP – THE M

The inspiration started on the lower step needs to be continued. However, here leaders need to start a process of MENTORING team members in order to MOTIVATE them to continue the journey. At this stage, certain team members will be much more committed to the process. The challenge of leadership is to create MOMENTUM and MOVEMENT towards the next level of embracing diversity.

THE TOP STEP – THE B

As we get to the top step, we will always see another set of steps that need climbing, but it's at this stage that we BUILD UP. We build up the relationships between people, we build up ourselves and the people around us. But to do that, we need to BREAK DOWN. We need to break down barriers, we need to break down walls between us. We need to break down the bias we show towards others.

Throughout this process, we need to realise that grand plans and visions of utopia are great as they provide leadership guidance. But the real challenge and understanding of leadership is that it is to move one person at a time, one group at a time and one organisation at a time.

And then we can really find ways of managing diversity in ways that benefit everyone. We get to BUILD UP ourselves, we get to build up our family, we get to build up our organisations. We get to build up our countries and we get to build up the world. We get to do this in ways that make the world a better place of harmony and diversity.

CHAPTER 9:

CREATE A FUN WORK ENVIRONMENT WITH A SERIOUS CULTURE

≈≈≈

One day when I retire I want forty years' experience, not one year forty times over.

ANON

I don't want to get to the end of my life and find that I just lived the length of it. I want to have lived the width of it as well.

DIANE ACKERMAN

Can a work environment be fun and serious at the same time? I believe it can! And I think the key is constant engagement. When taking a helicopter view of my current business, it seems totally mundane and very repetitive. If you look at it in the light of 'get application from client, send to bank, follow up with bank, settle loan' then it is indeed mundane and repetitive. However, reminding my team that there is a person or group of people on the end of every application and that each one of them is different and has different circumstances makes it both challenging and fun.

This chapter will cover:

- Being present in the business

- What makes an office a relaxed place?

- What are the rules for that culture?

- How do you manage that culture?

- What gives an office a serious culture?

- How do you maintain a serious culture in a relaxed environment?

When I look at the broking business, and as the team grew over the years, we tried to inculcate new staff into the relaxed culture, whilst all the time maintaining professional standards and ethics. There is an old saying about 'work hard and play hard' and that's probably the culture that myself and partners had always strived to create.

I have had to practice the distinct difference between being a control freak and 'being present'. You cannot successfully run a business without being present. There are numerous esteemed authors and academics who make the comments about working 'on the business not in the business'. Being present does not necessarily mean that you need to be working in the business. It means, in my terms, being involved in the day to day operations and being present with the operations.

In specific terms of the day-to-day mortgage business, it is necessary to understand the operations process overview to understand 'being present'. I spend a substantial portion of my time interviewing clients and then working out the relevant strategy for them. Once that part is done, my team take over. I mostly send the clients a detailed email with the strategy noted on it, and copy in my manager who then sends the client a list of required paperwork that needs to be signed, along with a list of documents that are required.

Once the client returns the paperwork, that file is allocated to one of the team who then starts the application process with the relevant lender and communicates the operational updates to the clients.

One of the best bits of business advice I was given was to get my business to a point where I can **delegate the $10 per hour tasks and concentrate on the $500/hour revenue**.

For me, my 'being present' means that I catch up with the team members for updates on their work flow a few times a week. At these catch up sessions all team members give updates to the rest of the team and myself. If any issues have arisen, then the team and I workshop and brainstorm the answers and viable solutions. This has many uses:

- It allows me to be present and have an update on all files and potential issues.

- It allows all team members to be part of the problem-solving process.

- It utilises our skills as a team and individually to problem-solve.

This example given above is the very serious business of me spending time with the team to review all the client files in their portfolio. The process is conducted by a meeting in the open plan space where all admin team members sit around and get a briefing from each of the team on each of their clients. This is often interspersed with jokes (possibly about the use of a word or phrase) or general comments about unrelated ideas. This repartee probably makes the meetings continue for longer than they should, but brings a certain lightness to a very serious process.

We are generally involved with clients making the largest financial transaction of their lives and to this end, we need to be mindful and respectful. However, if we just felt the pressure to perform and deliver, my team would crack. So, to share a joke, eat a chocolate and have general banter during a serious discussion is a good pressure release valve.

Being much more present in the operational aspect of the business does not require hands-on involvement in low level tasks, it rather requires the team member doing the lower level task, understanding their role and being appreciated for their role. The best way to show this appreciation is by engaging with them and allowing the team member to use you as a sounding board so that they feel part of the decision-making team process.

Many organisations refer to their structures as having open door policies. I have taken that to an extreme where the only time we close doors is when we are having client meetings in one of the interview rooms. My open-door policy means that my team will sometimes camp outside my office waiting for an opinion whilst I am busy (say on the phone). It's not uncommon for me to see a team member coming into my office with a pile of files in their hand. They often find that by bringing a specific subset of their work to discuss with me one-on-one helps them solve problems in a collaborative way.

Many years ago, we ended up with staff often working late into the night. As a rule, there were always a few cold beers in the fridge. The rule was simple, if you are working late and want a beer, please help yourself. BUT two rules – replace the cold beer with a warm one from the shelf and don't drink to excess and drive over the limit.

We always believed in treating the team like adults and not micro-managing all aspects of behaviour. I still don't clock-watch my team. If they need time off for personal reasons during a day, then they may arrange with other team members to cover them. Unless they take a full day, I don't expect leave applications or sick leave notes. But I do expect that they will make up the time at the first opportunity.

A telling aspect of the fun office culture is the number of practical jokes the staff play on each other – from the simple trick of hiding something such as a jumper or a teddy bear to the more elaborate. Every time one of the managers goes on extended leave he comes back to a desk that has been 'pimped'. After one trip the team covered his workspace in aluminum foil, including his chair. After another holiday he returned to his workspace having been converted to a cardboard fort, complete with windows and turrets.

One day, a series of wanted posters appeared around the office. We had been taking photos for use in advertising and broker profiles. One of the team convinced Aimee (doing our advertising and social media marketing) to Photoshop the manager's face onto a passport and make a wanted poster.

At the beginning of April in mid-2015, I was interviewing for a new receptionist. One of the admin team asked me if we could test the candidate's reactions by her staff member arriving at the interview dressed in a onesie (cow pattern). I thought that was probably a bit over the top and did not recommend it. However, the thought of doing it as a means of testing new staff and integrating them culturally was great and an indication of team spirit.

One of the simplest rules that I try and reinforce daily is communication. My staff and I receive many calls during the day and sometimes we want a message taken to avoid interruption. I will generally strive to ensure that all return calls are made the same day. If it's late, I may SMS the person who left a message and say something along the lines of 'hi, it's late and I did not want to call. If it's urgent we can chat now or is tomorrow ok?'

The serious culture impacts the expected level of communication required from staff, for example how to make the 'hard calls'. A hard call is one of those calls to a client to give them bad news – potentially that their loan has been declined. If I need to make one of those calls, I always make them from the open plan work space where all the team members can hear how I am dealing with the client. I would say that in 90% of cases, I try and find a positive spin. This may be as simple as 'you need to save more money for a deposit so let's catch up on the phone the first Monday of every month to see how your savings are going'. However, it is often more complex where a loan has been declined on some technical policy level and my job is to explain that to the client in layman's terms, whilst at the same time (hopefully) giving them an alternative solution.

That second part of the conversation is a vital aspect of the communication with the client as it allows us to put a positive spin on the unwelcome news by providing an alternative that perhaps works for the client. Also, it provides the staff with some significant training in customer relations.

〜〜〜

Years ago, I was advised that the origin of the male necktie was to hide buttons. These buttons were made from bone and discoloured over time. It was regarded as an insult to 'show someone your discoloured buttons' and hence the necktie was born. I'm never sure if this is the correct origin, but I use that story to justify why I don't wear a tie.

Part of the relaxed office culture is that no one in the office has ever worn a tie on a regular basis. I don't believe that customers care whether the person talking to them is smartly dressed or formally dressed in a tie, or for that matter wearing a 'company branded' polo shirt. So, in all my businesses though first impressions do count, the overall impression, tempered by knowledge and attitude to the client, will prevail.

CHAPTER 10

KEEP IT SIMPLE

≈≈≈

If you find yourself in a hole, the first thing to do is stop digging.

WILL ROGERS

This chapter addresses the idea that business is not complicated – by **keeping it simple** it is possible to create success.

During my Engineering studies, we had a lecturer in physics who embodied the principle of keeping it simple. Physics is not simple by nature and the principles we were learning were incredibly complex.

However, this lecturer had a way of teaching that made this complex subject become simple to understand. He was totally focused on making life simple. He always spoke about the fact that in complex mathematics there are two basic methodologies used – differentiation and integration. In simple terms each is the reverse procedure of the other – 'I only know how to differentiate – I just reverse the process to integrate, as I like to keep my life simple'. The mathematics lecturers would have dealt with both methods as separate with separate methods and protocols.

What always stayed with me was that even in this completely complex subject of physics, he managed to find ways to simplify life.

EDUCATION IS ABOUT LEARNING TO THINK

I am often asked what I learned in my years of study towards two master's degrees. I always answer that I learned to think. I am obviously a major fan of education, but I believe that any education must have as its core philosophy teaching people to think. The knowledge base is less important than the skills learned.

Between my MBA and starting the IMD education business I spent around 18 months working at a highly technical software company in a marketing and business development role. However, there were times when I needed to get involved in writing software code if deadlines were approaching, and the team was short staffed. My approach of keeping it simple was a significant bone of contention.

The Company, Kenwalt, had developed some very sophisticated simulation software, running on PCs that could simulate the operation of a chemical or industrial plant. By way of explanation, flight simulator software is probably the closest equivalent that most people have seen today. However, this was back in 1989 and 1990 when the computing power of the PC was very limited.

WATCH FOR POINTS OR NO GAIN FOR EFFORT

One of my good friends, an incredibly clever chemical engineer, would spend days and weeks writing complex formulae to simulate the operation of aspects of an industrial plant that we were modelling. I came along to help, and suggested that we simplify the models in areas where the actual operational process was not critical to the operation, (as opposed to chemical reaction models that by their very nature are complex). As an example, Adrian had spent days writing the model of a circular water tank and how it filled up and emptied. I looked at this and said, **'keep it simple'** if we open the valve at the top it fills up in pretty much a straight line and when you open the valve at the bottom it empties. If both valves are open the water level will change depending on which valve is open more. I then wrote a simple model of the tank in a day that became part of the overall model of the plant. The continuing debate was whether my model was strictly accurate, which it was not. However, it did the job, and more importantly it didn't detract from the overall model.

How does this work in business? We tend to spend a lot of time working on the aspects of the business that don't really add value. There is a point of nil return where more effort and refinement does not yield significant advantages.

Recently an associate put a message on social media asking for comment on which version of a logo looked better. I thought that I would consider the options and send some feedback. The changes were so subtle that I needed to look a few times to see the variances. Her focus at that instant was on the differences and not the substance, and whether the subtle differences made a difference. In my opinion, she forgot to keep it simple.

In the mortgage business, I am often told that I explain structures and strategies to clients in ways that are easy for them to understand. The way I explain has evolved from the way that I started in the industry. I came into the finance broking space from a position of never having worked in a bank or banking environment. The norm was, and still is, that most finance brokers emanate from the banking world. In that world, the use of TLAs (three-letter acronyms) is prevalent and buzzwords are the norm. This tends to make simple explanations quite complex for the consumer.

The fact that I had to try and understand this world myself without having been immersed in the culture of complex buzzwords and acronyms meant that the explanations I found cut through the jargon and are still valid and relevant today.

I took a completely contrarian approach, one that still works today. When any of the team interviews a client, it is done using pen and paper (or note taking iPad software). This essentially allows the team member to establish with the client that they know what they are talking about and reinforces their credibility as they are not relying on the software for the answer. Part of this pen and paper approach has evolved into a series of very simple graphical sketches that we use to demonstrate the loan structure and strategy. I keep on my desk a set of coloured pens and highlighters. Using simple colour coding I am able to draw out a complex structure using simple terms and pictures that everyone can understand. This process and method has a twofold advantage – it reinforces the broker credibility by showing how knowledgeable the broker is and it keeps it simple.

I have always been one to find a simple solution to a complex problem. One of the most pressing and challenging problems in the mortgage business is that of workflow and workflow management.

Human nature is such that we tend to push the hard tasks away and focus on the easy ones. I realised this as the mortgage business grew and my support team grew. My back-office team would deal with the easy files regularly and push the complex ones further and further down the pile of active client files.

I had worked out that my average assistant could work with 20-30 files at any time. If they touched each file twice a week that would be a maximum of 60 files per week or 12 per day. From this I developed a basic scheduling system called Monday to Friday. Each person has a set of shelves labelled Monday through Friday and a whiteboard with five columns labelled the same.

Starting on a Monday they pick up a file and contact the relevant bank. The banks say we will answer you on Thursday. They take the file, put it on the Thursday shelf and write the clients name in the Thursday column on the whiteboard.

This means that once the system is working, the staff member does not face a daunting pile of files each day but a maximum of 12 and more regularly around 8 to deal with in a day.

One of my assistants, several years ago, before the advent of the system, used to joke that if her pile of files fell over she would resign before they hit the ground. The Monday to Friday system solved that as the pile was greatly reduced each day.

In addition, when a staff member calls in sick, it's easy to reallocate their work for the day as it is clearly defined and delineated.

This simple system allowed the staff to take control of their workflow by not facing a mound of work each day. They gave up control of all the files daily to get control of their day-to-day lives.

Chapter 11
The End of the Beginning

There is an ancient quote that paraphrased says that it is not about the destination, it's is about the journey.

My experience of writing this book has been an amazing journey in trying to piece together 30+ years of experience.

It has been a journey to understand the forces that have shaped my business ideas and principles.

It has been a journey to appreciate the wisdom and council of those who have offered their time and knowledge to me on my way.

The journey as an entrepreneur has been fun, exciting, scary and empowering.

I started this book describing the epiphany of diving in. The idea of never being totally prepared for everything in life and realising that to be successful in business you have

to accept that sometimes you have to dive in and see what happens.

Closing this chapter is an end, but also the beginning of the next chapter in my journey.

My journey continues as a speaker and educator, passing on my passion for business. I want to share my experience, I want to pay it forward, I want to reward those who helped me by helping others. I'm diving into a new business journey of GIVE your business the EDGE.

I hope you enjoyed swimming along with me.

Good luck on your journey. Dive in!

RB

ACKNOWLEDGEMENTS

Getting to the point of publishing this book has been with help and support of a number of people:

Aimee and Rafi for being my first proofreaders and putting up with the really bad English and grammar.

Batya Bricker for taking a rambling story and making it into a book.

All my colleagues and mentors as professional speakers who encouraged me to pursue my passion.

All my business partners and colleagues over the years who have shared with me their passion for business and success.

About Rael Bricker

Rael Bricker is a collector of experiences and observations. With over 30 years as an entrepreneur, he delivers a series of dynamic workshops on building businesses by thinking outside the norm. His experiences range from working 6000 feet underground, building an education business with six campuses and 4000 students, several years in venture capital and his financial services group with more than $2.8Bn in settled residential loans. Rael has been involved in listed companies on two stock exchanges and sees himself as a 'serial entrepreneur'. Rael has spent many years in community and not for profit leadership positions and sees that as one aspect of 'paying it forward'.

His focus is on taking businesses in any industry and making them larger and more successful by enabling the owners and operators to look at their businesses through different lenses.

Rael Bricker holds two Masters degrees, an MBA and MSc (engineering) and is currently a Fellow of the MFAA (Mortgage and Finance Association of Australia) and a Member of PSA (Professional Speakers Australia).

Rael has been presenting for many years on a variety of topics related to property, investing and business. These are an accumulation of experiences where the common thread is that they weave a unique perspective on small and medium business and business development. This has evolved into Rael's current business (2018) called 'Give your Business the EDGE' where he delivers keynote addresses and workshops centered around a large portion of the material in this book.

Testimonials

On keynote presentations:

'Rael brought a thoughtful, intelligent and heartfelt address to the Vow Financial Conference in Whistler, Canada. Rael's ability to present and weave stories that are thought-provoking and motivating is artistry in motion. Myself and more than 200 guests were compelled by Rael's business and management insights and the message of following your dream and staying true to yourself. Rael is a charismatic and inspirational person, listening and meeting Rael was truly an uplifting and positive experience, his perspective on issues was a breath of fresh air. Rael, has made a lasting impact on my life, and am sure many others as well.' *Stephen Lambert Senior Financial Planner – Crown Wealth Group.*

'I was extremely interested in what Rael had to say and he gave me many ideas on how to "work smarter - not harder" '

'His method of presentation made the session extremely interesting and really is the sort of guy you could listen to all day.'

'I found it to be valuable insight and certainly felt Rael was humble'.

'Really enjoyed this session. A lot of very helpful tips and advice to take on and consider. I think more sessions like Rael's would be great. Hearing from top brokers who have built successful businesses. How they did it and what to avoid'.

'Really appreciated his frankness and willingness to share his experiences and what worked for him. Now I'm looking for the blue ocean'

'I want to thank you very much for the excellent presentation you gave at the CEO breakfast meeting. I am looking forward to your book, do you have a waiting/mailing list? If so, can you please add me to it'.

'I found Rael's presentation very relevant as it resonated with my experiences as a CEO'.

'Rael hit a chord because I found his presentation full of practical and real advice that made me think there were some things I'd done well, and other areas that I could do better'.

ON TECHNICAL PRESENTATIONS:

'I have heard Rael present at professional meetings, seminars, workshops and conferences over 100 times. He's a regular presenter and greatly sought after and is invited interstate over a dozen times each year. Rael engages with the audience and has the rare ability to break complex financial issues into the layman's language. It's fascinating to see the audience respond to him and enjoy his presentations. He is never dull. Despite having heard him over 100 times I find he rarely repeats himself, changing the presentations content and style to suit the audience. He speaks with great passion and a sense of humour so that he never loses the audience. His presentations are always interesting and infor-mative. The fact that he's always sought after to present at various forums is a testament to his skills' *Harpal Ahluwalia – Branch Manager – Property Club*

'We are Australia's biggest property marketing group, the Property Club and bring education to property buyers. The problem is that this education covers a multitude of complex areas from estate planning, managing multiple investments through to responding to ever changing legislation. No matter which topic we choose for Rael he is always most obliging in taking on the task. He returns with a fully researched presentation and has the unique skill of reducing a very technical presentation down to simple concepts that are readily absorbed by the audience. Rael has the ability to use minimal but effective power points to achieve this transfer of knowledge. We are very pleased with Rael's results when we survey our members post conference. Rael has one of the highest survey results of "did you get" the presentation. Uniquely Rael loves the open question and answer sessions at the end of his presentations. He revels in the challenge of answering the most difficult of questions and again in a way where the audience say "got that"! We recommend Rael as a most professional presenter with exceptional speaking skills. We have had a long list of well-known economic and property celebrities at our conferences over the last 23 years. Rael continually rates right up there with these speakers.' *Kevin Young - President of Property Club.*

ON BEING MASTER OF CEREMONIES:

'We hold an annual conference to bring our large membership together. The highlight of this is the Saturday evening dinner with a live band or an orchestra. We are very grateful that Rael Bricker has provided his MC services to us for each of the seven years. This is a vital role to see that the evening runs smoothly and with the right amount of humour. Rael handles this difficult job with professional ease. Rael continues to earn this task by popular demand from our members. No matter which city we hold the event in Rael always makes himself available and is a font of knowledge on assisting in the organisational effort prior to the event. I am more than happy to recommend Rael as an MC for any event.' *Kevin Young - President of Property Club.*

"Rael has done an outstanding job as an MC, wowing the audience and engaging them with jokes and anecdotes whilst ensuring the events flow along beautifully within the time frames. The feedback from attendees has been excellent. Rael is an absolute professional and a delight, no wonder he is called upon every year to be the MC.'